FABIO GURGEL

UNSHAKEABLE

JIU-JITSU LEADERSHIP PRINCIPLES APPLIED TO LIFE AND BUSINESS

FABIO GURGEL

UNSHAKEABLE

JIU-JITSU LEADERSHIP PRINCIPLES APPLIED TO LIFE AND BUSINESS

São Paulo | 2025

Título: *Unshakeable: Jiu-Jitsu leadership principles applied to life and business*

The opinions and comments made in this publication are personal and do not necessarily represent the opinion of the institutions to which the authors are linked.
The rights to this edition belong to LVM Editora, headquartered at
Avenida das Nações Unidas, Nº 18.801 - 4th Floor - Room 407
Jardim Dom Bosco - São Paulo-SP - Zip Code: 04757-025
contato@lvmeditora.com.br

Editor-in-Chief | Pedro Henrique Alves
Assistant editors | Geizy Novais and Felipe Saraiça
Spelling and grammar check | Thuany Priscila Zuanazzi
Originals preparation | Adriana Alevato, Marcio Scansani, Damian Hirtz and Pedro Henrique Alves
Cover and graphic design | Mariângela Ghizellini
Cover photo | André Schiliró
Layout | Décio Lopes

International Cataloging-in-Publication Data (CIP)
Angélica Ilacqua CRB-8/7057

G987n Gurgel, Fabio
Unshakeable: Jiu-Jitsu leadership principles applied to life and business / Fabio Gurgel. - 1ª edição - São Paulo : LVM Editora, 2025.
256 p.

ISBN 978-65-5052-272-8

1. Jiu-jítsu 2. Figth (sport) 3. Gurgel, Fabio, 1953 4. Martial fighters I. Title

24-4548 CDD 796.8152

Indexes to systematic catalog:
1. Jiu-jítsu

Summary

Presentation

Master Romero "Jacaré" Cavalcanti[1]

Fabio Gurgel is more than a jiu-jitsu athlete or teacher; he is a true visionary, whose determination and passion have been instrumental in turning modern jiu-jitsu into a worldwide phenomenon. It's a privilege, as his master for over 40 years, to witness this trajectory and the positive impact it has had on so many around the world.

I was proud to meet Fabio as a teenager and to see, over the decades, his tireless dedication to jiu-jitsu and the values that the sport teaches. He has become an extraordinary human being, guided by principles of honor, loyalty and discipline – virtues that define him both on and off the mats. Seeing Fabio apply these values in life and in business is inspiring, and his example reflects everything that jiu-jitsu stands for.

In *Unshakeable,* Fabio shares the lessons, challenges and victories that have shaped his journey. This book is an invaluable guide for anyone seeking strength and resilience, whether in sport, business or life.

1. Master 8th degree, Red and White belt.

Foreword

Roberto Altenhofen

With all due respect, but this isn't my space. It belongs to Jacaré, Rickson, Gigi... Maybe Demian, Jocko and even Mark Kerr. From there up".

That's how I first turned down the invitation to be here, addressing you.

The answer I received was straight:

"I disagree! These are important but obvious characters. I think their view from the outside – and then from the inside – sends a message much more in line with what I want to achieve with my book."

But what is the book about?

What does he want to achieve?

***

I was in an extremely uncomfortable situation.

I was one of the spectators at a course on management for jiu-jitsu academies, which was taking place in a hotel in São Paulo. I was opening a jiu-jitsu academy in the same area as the Alliance Jiu-jitsu headquarters, in the Vila Olímpia district of São Paulo.

Although I practiced and loved martial arts, I wasn't an athlete, I wasn't a professional fighter and I wasn't a teacher either. My role there was basically that of an investor; I was making possible what was a dream of my teacher at the time.

As it was my first investment in the business, I went there to understand what I was getting myself into. What's more, I was going to learn some of the secrets of what would soon be my competitor in the region: Fabio Gurgel, the host of the event.

Like all practitioners, I knew the stories of the Alliance's "General"; the four-time black belt world champion, the thick-skinned man who was at the forefront of the old jiu-jitsu challenges against other martial arts, which were fundamental to consolidating the brand of the "most efficient fighting system in the world", the fighter from the early days of bare-knuckle vale-tudo, then the UFC and, above all, the leader of the biggest and winningest team of jiu-jitsu competitors in the world.

I arrived at the hotel with a deep curiosity about that character. I left admiring a manager.

The course was incredible, with many insights that I could apply not only in my gym, but also in my personal life and in my main business, the financial market.

At the end of the almost three-hour event, I went to greet the professor briefly: "Congratulations, Fabio. What you've shown here needs to reach a lot more people – and I think I can help you with that. Here's my card. If you're interested, we can have a coffee in my office to discuss it".

Fabio greeted me cordially. At that point, he had no idea what my real intention was with that gesture...

In fact, I had a genuine interest in helping him promote his gym management product, but I had a bigger problem to deal with first. I was about to open a competing gym a block away from his school, starting what could be a competition for space and students in the area – and I decided that the best thing to do was to tell him about it in person.

Since there was some risk of things getting ugly, I figured that I would minimize any possible damage if we were in a controlled environment – in this case, my office.

When he arrived at the office on Avenida Faria Lima, we went to a meeting room. I chose a glass room, with transparent walls, where outsiders could see us, although not hear us, and I immediately took the weight off my back: "Fabio, first of all, I need to be honest with you. I'm opening a gym under a different brand in Vila Olímpia, so I went to your gym management course".

"Exactly where is this gym of yours going to be?" – he answered immediately.

So I tried to distance the location as much as possible... I argued that I didn't know the surrounding streets very well, but when we opened the map on my cell phone, I couldn't fight it.

"Well, it'll be right next to my gym. Up the block!" – he concluded.

At that moment, I realized that the worst was just around the corner. My heart rate rose abruptly and I looked through the glass, hoping there would be people standing by outside the room, to which he added: "That's excellent news. I'm glad to know that you'll have someone capable nearby. Someone who will be able to offer the students a good level of service".

Surprised, I interrupted him: "Wait. Let me get this straight... This isn't a problem for you?".

To which he promptly replied:

"You know what's a problem for me? It's the infinite number of badly-run, dirty gyms, with teachers who treat students badly, who are late for class, who teach with dirty gi's, who don't speak properly and who, in this way, diminish jiu-jitsu. Once they go there, the student has an extremely negative experience, to the point of never coming back; either to that or any other jiu-jitsu academy. I'm really happy that you have a good project for the region".

It was a shock. That reaction went head-on against the sport's entire history of raids on rival gyms, brawls in championships and conflicts between practitioners of different flags.

From that moment on, I realized that I wouldn't be able to fight (commercially) in the region, but I gained a teacher, a reference, later a partner in another project and, even more importantly, someone I now consider a friend.

This brief passage is a summary of what I understand to be Fabio Gurgel's purpose: to show jiu-jitsu outside of jiu-jitsu.

What you'll find in the following pages is a man on a mission. A noble and very successful mission, with remarkable feats, surprising events and emblematic characters; but, above all, you will find the man, an interlocutor who is mixed up between practitioner, athlete, fighter, teacher, leader, coach, entrepreneur and eternal student – with his due failures, dilemmas, learnings, and his incessant search for virtue.

Everything is here. The relationship with Master Jacaré, the rise as an athlete, the founding of Alliance, the transitions in his career, the split in the team, the pain for his friend Marcelo Behring, the injuries, the world titles, the training with Carlson, the respect for Rickson, the clash with Mark Kerr, the fight to professionalize the sport, the development of the business model and the teaching methodology...

Unshakeable aims to show that the world's most efficient fight is also one of the most powerful tools for personal development. And it achieves this through a courageous, passionate and, above all, necessary account of one of the people who, to this day, has best understood the true size of the gentle art, far beyond the mats.

Take off your shoes. Tie your belt. Go to the center of the mat, greet the General and...

Happy reading!

△

Introduction

One day in 1985, sitting in the living room of our apartment in Ipanema, Rio de Janeiro, I was listening to my father and Fernando – my older brother – discussing his professional future, since he had just been approved to study engineering at the Pontifical Catholic University of Rio de Janeiro (PUC-RJ). I don't remember the details of the conversation; after all, I wasn't the subject, nor did I have any knowledge to give an opinion. Happy to be in their company, I just listened until my father asked what I would do when I grew up. "Jiu-jitsu," I replied.

Jokingly, he commented: "I'm referring to work".

"Me too," I said at once.

The conversation turned in my direction and the atmosphere became heavier. Work was a very serious matter at home, and my father had always been our greatest example of commitment and sacrifice; of "doing what needs to be done".

"Are you going to work with jiu-jitsu? Do you have any idea how big that market is? If you choose engineering, law or medicine, which are careers with a large established market, you will obviously have more job opportunities. Jiu-Jitsu, on the other hand, seems to me to have very few possibilities. Do you really think you can be good and stand out in this market?"

At the age of fifteen, I replied: "I think I can be very good, and I love doing jiu-jitsu".

"If you believe that, I'll just say two things: first, you'll have to work very hard. Then you have to look ahead, be able to think differently from the majority. If the market opens up and you keep that in mind, you'll certainly be able to find your place."

I grew up with this conversation in my head, a guide for me to dedicate myself to being the best I could be, not to settle for any achievement, to keep my eyes ahead and see the opportunities that would come along. I had to be different!

Much of what has happened to me to this day didn't even cross my mind at the time of that conversation, when I categorically stated that I wanted to do jiu-jitsu for a living. I couldn't have imagined getting so far or learning so much from this martial art.

Among the greatest lessons I've learned is undoubtedly the importance of sharing my knowledge. This happened to me very naturally and – unfortunately, most of the time – imperceptibly. And it took me a long time to be able to explain why I had this passion for teaching and sharing.

A few years ago, I had the opportunity to teach a great expert in the world of marketing, an extremely successful American, writer of more than a dozen books, and a black belt in jiu-jitsu: Mark Ford. He told me that one of the tactics he used constantly in marketing was to share strategies and knowledge, which he had learned in jiu-jitsu.

It's common to train with the same group, so that your opponents – in a way – know your strengths and weaknesses. Without the exchange of knowledge and insights, training will stagnate.

Sharing is at the heart of "being a teacher", but I believe that everyone should use it as a source of self-development.

According to common sense, by sharing, we diminish a competitive advantage. For example, if every day I practice with a certain partner and apply the same armlock[2] , I'll

2. A movement in which you force your opponent's joint using a lever created with your own body.

have the sweet satisfaction of victory, without any challenge. If I share with him the points that make him vulnerable to such a technique, I will improve my opponent. In return, I'll also make my own path more difficult. However, on closer inspection, it's easy to see that, as well as doing my training partner good, I'll be forcing my own development – now I'll have to use another technique, another tactic to win.

It seems obvious that if I have a dispute – be it a fight or a business strategy – telling my opponent what to do is not the smartest course of action. On the other hand, believing that the same attitude will work forever is just as dangerous, as it leads you to close yourself off to evolution and possible attacks on your position.

How many empires have fallen, how many companies have closed down and how many champions have been overtaken because they insisted on doing things the same way, following what "has always worked"?

As counterintuitive as it may seem, sharing forces you to evolve while challenging your opponents to study your past tactics. This keeps you ahead of the game, looking to the future, constantly renewing, and benefiting everyone around you.

Genuine help doesn't have to be altruistic; there's no sin in doing good to yourself. As long as ethical and moral concepts are strictly followed, sharing knowledge makes everyone better off, including you.

In *The Virtue of Selfishness*, the Russian-born American author and philosopher Ayn Rand classifies altruism as one of humanity's great problems, which leads us further away from the truth and into an almost inevitable hypocrisy.

On the other hand, doing good for others is a basic condition for discovering the real meaning of life. Walking or achieving any goal alone doesn't seem like a good strategy in our eternal search for purpose. So why not be true to ourselves and align these concepts?

Another Russian philosopher, Fyodor Dostoevsky, when dealing with the *"dialectic of vanity"*, proposes directing our interests in such a way as to do good to others at the same time as we do it to ourselves[3].

We need to understand that it's not possible to take the ego out of the equation – the ego is us. The question is how to accommodate it in relation to the other things around us. By putting too much attention on it, we become insensitive, unbearable egolaters and, even if we win, we may face loneliness and false friendships, which definitely don't make for a happy life. On the other hand, not taking care of our ego and wanting to live totally focused on others goes against basic human nature – taking care of ourselves – which ends up forcing us to live divided between two characters: the altruistic one, which we show to others in search of acceptance and admiration, and our true self, out of the spotlight, with vanities and needs that we try to hide as much as possible from others.

In my forty-year jiu-jitsu journey, I've had to learn to deal with this athlete-teacher duality. To be a champion, you need a large dose of selfishness – there is only one winner in every contest. On the other hand, in the role of teacher, everything must be done for the student, in other words, for others.

I had to navigate these two parallel worlds at the same time from a very young age, training to win and working with people who often had different goals in jiu-jitsu. Aligning these paths is what brought me here, allowing me to learn some important lessons that I intend to share with you over the next few pages.

I don't know if this will be considered a book about jiu-jitsu, but I hope to be able to help those who are already practicing to apply the concepts of the art, as well as arouse the curiosity and interest of those who haven't put on the kimono yet.

Get ready. It's worth it!

---

3. According to the author Joseph Frank, in the book *Dostoevsky: a writer in his time,* published in Brazil by Editora Companhia das Letras.

CHAPTER 1
The story

"History is written by the victors," says the famous phrase attributed to George Orwell, pseudonym of Eric Arthur Blair, author of *1984* and *Animal Farm*, two great dystopian novels.

Events are told over time in different ways, and the knowledge passed down from generation to generation is part of humanity's evolution – no matter whether it's transmitted in practical, narrated or written form. The veracity of events is reserved only for those who experienced them, although the way they are told can completely influence future generations and thus the world as we know it.

When we reflect on the popular saying "he who tells a tale raises a point", we notice that the older the story, the further away from the truth we are – we can imagine a geometric progression of how far we can be from the fact itself as time goes by. As such, the search for truth remains one of man's great challenges.

In the cradle of Western Civilization, the great thinkers of Ancient Greece, especially those known as pre-Socratics – such as Thales of Miletus, Heraclitus of Ephesus and Parmenides – tried to discover the reason for things, to understand the truths of the world through *physis*, the study of nature.

Socrates, known as the father of philosophy, sought to understand man, living together in society, justice, morality and truth. He, who defined himself through the maxim "I only know that I know nothing", disputed the stage with the Sophists, a group of thinkers who had rhetoric and the power of argument as their main characteristics, and who opposed the concept of a single truth – for them, there is a consensus version of events.

I understand that history is often divided: on the one hand, proven accounts; on the other, narratives that, having been told so much by victorious or dominant agents of the time, become "axioms" – even if they don't accurately represent the facts – and boast the power to influence generations.

The history of jiu-jitsu – as it was told at the time, in the early 1980s – was undoubtedly romanticized and narrated by winners, since the Gracie family completely dominated the sports scene in Rio de Janeiro. I repeat here exactly what they told me and, consequently, influenced me throughout my journey.

The story begins in Japan at the beginning of the 20th century, at the end of the Meiji era. The opening of Japanese ports to the West allowed for a large migration of Japanese to the Americas, including Brazil.

During one of these immigrations, a fighter and champion, Mitsuyo Maeda, nicknamed Count Koma, arrived in Belém do Pará. Gastão Gracie, an influential businessman, helped the Japanese community to settle in the city and, as a way of showing his gratitude, Maeda offered to teach jiu-jitsu to his eldest son, Carlos Gracie, on the condition that the young man kept the teachings a secret. The transformation of that undisciplined teenager was visible. He started attending the master's classes, took great care of his health and fulfilled all his responsibilities.

Years later, the Gracie family moved to Rio de Janeiro, and the young Carlos began to teach the martial art to his four younger brothers – Oswaldo, George, Gastão Jr. and Hélio – and they began to challenge the city's fighters in order to prove the efficiency of jiu-jitsu.

With the success of their fights, they founded the Gracie academy in 1925 in Rio de Janeiro. The family gained notoriety through the fights of Carlos and, later, Oswaldo and George – nicknamed Gato Ruivo for his agility and technique. Carlos was the brothers' mentor and leader.

Conflicts began to arise when George began to be invited to vale tudo fights, which were very common at the time, and Carlos vehemently disagreed. Their relationship broke down, and George went on a trip through Brazil, taking jiu-jitsu mainly to the interior of São Paulo, while Oswaldo helped spread the sport in Minas Gerais.

The story goes that Hélio Gracie, a frail and sickly young man who felt dizzy, was forbidden by his doctor to do any physical activity. A great admirer of his older brother, he always attended his classes and, in this way, became familiar with his techniques. One day, Carlos was late and Hélio, who was at the gym, received someone offering to train him instead of his brother. The student accepted and, in the end, asked Carlos to take his classes with Hélio – now his teacher – from that day on.

After George and Oswaldo separated, Hélio became the family's main fighter, under the mentorship of Carlos, who chose his opponents, set challenges and promoted the name of the Gracie academy throughout the city.

Hélio became the big name in the family and revolutionized the techniques learned until then, adapting his slight physique to the efficiency of the movements, applying the principle leverage to reduce the need for physical strength.

Hélio Gracie's achievements are historic and his bravery undeniable. No time limit fights with much stronger and heavier opponents, combined with an unshakable self-confidence in his technique and jiu-jitsu, made him the greatest fighter in Brazil at the time.

Two fights, two losses are the most famous stories told about Hélio Gracie.

The first came after his choke victory over world runner-up Yukio Kato, a condition set by world judo champion Masahiko Kimura to accept the challenge proposed by Hélio.

In October 1951, Kimura and Hélio fought at the Maracanã stadium in a bout that lasted thirteen minutes. The Japanese fighter, who was 31 kilos heavier than Hélio, had commented that his opponent could be considered the winner if he lasted more than three minutes.

The second fight took place in 1955, and was considered by Hélio to be a brawl, as it was against a former black belt student, Waldemar Santana, who was also an employee of the Gracie academy – fired after forgetting to turn off the taps and almost flooding the academy.

A while later, Hélio allowed him to rejoin the student body, but a proposal to fight in a place where mixed style fights had historically taken place brought the conflict between the two to the surface once again. Hélio Gracie didn't agree with Waldemar's participation and expelled him once again.

Infuriated by the people around him, the former student challenged the master. To this day, the fight ranks as the longest in history, and came to an end after around three hours, when an exhausted forty-two-year-old Hélio fell and took a final kick to the face.

A year after that fight, the successor to the Gracie family came on the scene. Considered by many to be the best fighter of all time, Carlson avenged his uncle Hélio in a historic moment at Maracanãzinho. He went on to face Waldemar Santana several more times, as well as dozens of other fighters, and was never defeated.

With Carlson as their main fighter and Hélio as their teacher, the Gracie family followed the tradition and spread their fame throughout Brazil.

In the 1970s, Carlson set up his own space in Copacabana, alongside his younger brother Rolls, Carlos' son who had been raised by Hélio and was already considered the family's new champion.

At that time, Romero Jacaré Cavalcanti – who became my master in 1985 – returned to jiu-jitsu to train with Toninho and Rolls. From then on, the story came to me almost entirely from him.

Jiu-jitsu championships began to take place between high schools, mainly those located in the suburbs of Rio de Janeiro and which had a slightly different lineage from the Gracie academy – they were students of master Fadda.

Hélio's, Carlson's and Rolls' academies held internal selections among their students, and the best represented them in tournaments.

In 1982, a tragic hang-gliding accident took Rolls' life at the age of thirty-three. Just six months earlier, Jacaré had graduated as the legendary master's sixth and final black belt.

After Rolls passed away, another leader emerged as the family's number one. Rickson, who had just passed a litmus test in a fight in Brasilia against the feared King Zulu, was ready to take over.

This is a concise summary of what happened and who were the main characters in jiu-jitsu when I started training in the second half of 1983. These are facts that still enchant me, as they tell of the bravery and courage of the Gracie family fighters in the process of training their students, many of whom are still famous – João Alberto Barreto, Pedro Hemetério, Hélio Vígio and many others. Their stories aroused my admiration and fueled my desire to be part of that world.

Under the guidance of master Hélio and with Rickson being the great champion, Carlson emerged as the best teacher, training a huge number of victors.

Jiu-Jitsu has grown a lot in these forty years, and all the attempts to challenge the story told by the Gracie family – why not say "by the winners"? – has never prospered. There are divergent narratives told by Carlson, and even some fights within the family, but effective leadership doesn't seem to be an issue.

In 2008, Reila, daughter of master Carlos and mother of champion Roger Gracie, realized that her father's image was being erased from history as the founder of the martial art in Brazil. She decided to write *Carlos Gracie: The Creator of a Fighting Dynasty*, a book that dropped like a bombshell in the jiu-jitsu community and displeased many members of the family because it exposed intimacies and told a much less romanticized version of the others. Without detracting from Hélio's brilliance as a fighter and teacher, she made it clear that the main steps and effective leadership were always in the hands of Carlos, who instructed him in absolutely everything. It also deconstructed the idea that Hélio had never trained until he became a teacher, among other points.

As jiu-jitsu has continued to grow and has taken over the United States and the world, the eyes of many historians have turned to the search for the truth about its trajectory in Brazil. Today, we see many more characters and perceive many more details.

In *Muito Antes Do MMA [Long before MMA]*, historians Elton Silva and Eduardo Corrêa have done extensive research since the first fighting events in Brazil at the beginning of the 20th century, collecting rich documents on the influence of other fighting styles, the path taken by the main fighters and their connections, who learned from whom, how they were formed and what the most important lineages of martial arts in Brazil are.

The Gracie family has cultivated a legion of students, fighters and fans, defenders of the values of jiu-jitsu, admirers of the courage, bravery and respect shown over decades of fighting, which proves its superiority as a martial art.

Not accepting matched fights, which are likely to tarnish the honor of jiu-jitsu and what it stands for, has also developed the opposite feeling in many opponents. Defeated in the ring and even outside of it, they have nurtured a rivalry and tried to dispute history, without being able to prove anything that changes the fact that jiu-jitsu is the most efficient form of fighting.

I grew up under the aura of invincibility created by my family. Hearing that a jiu-jitsu fighter weighing over 80 kilos was invincible was undoubtedly essential in the development of my self-confidence. The technique I learned and the way it was taught confirmed my feeling that we are capable of anything.

As I said at the beginning of this chapter, there are different accounts of the same story. The facts can be described exactly as they happened, romanticized or even transformed, but the description I have come to know has greatly shaped the man I am.

CHAPTER 2

The beginning

My childhood was filled with sports and competitions. From an early age, I always took part in tournaments at the Federal Club in Rio de Janeiro. My parents encouraged me and my siblings to venture into different sports and the club held an annual Olympics, in which members were divided into five or six teams to compete in absolutely everything – table tennis, skating, soccer, swimming, basketball, snooker, athletics, etc. It was a lot of fun and we had the opportunity to try out several different sports – often on the same day – and earn points for the team. It was a big party during the month of July.

Competing among friends from an early age and trying out different sports made me understand my abilities and skills, as well as which activities were more difficult for me.

The years went by and the competitions began to move away from the controlled sphere of a club, where I knew practically all the members and staff, to tournaments with outside guests.

In soccer, our team often played against the city's schools. We trained twice a week and played on Saturdays. Our coach – and my first teacher – was Carlinhos, a well-known former player for Flamengo (a soccer club in Rio de Janeiro), who went on to become coach and Brazilian Serie A champion years later for the same team.

I was skillful and one of the highlights of the team. One day, I complained that a teammate was repeatedly passing me the ball the wrong way, and I received the following lesson from the teacher: "Do you think things should always happen the way you want them to? When something goes wrong, do you want to blame the other person? It's your job to control the ball however it comes. Stop complaining about others and do your own thing!"

Carlinhos was always on the edge of the pitch. He was a leader who played with the team, he really cared, and that made us want to deliver the result, something beyond our will alone. His commitment was undoubtedly a very important motivational factor in sport and I, who have always fought for something greater, found this understanding by practicing a collective activity.

Soccer accompanied me throughout my childhood and early adolescence, and all the other sports went hand in hand with it. At a certain time, public tennis courts were built at Aterro do Flamengo and Lagoa, where I took lessons. I remember that, right at the start, the teacher had the group of about ten children line up with both hands on the racket, as if we were waiting for the ball. He gave the command for us to position ourselves for a *forehand* right smash[4]. The whole class went to the right and I went to the left – my dominant hand. I heard the teacher shout: "Didn't you hear me say right?"

I quickly shook my head in agreement and switched hands to play tennis with my right hand. Thanks to my ambidextrousness, this wasn't a problem and I learned, through sports, how to make the most of this condition.

Tennis became my focus for a few years. I played in tournaments and my father started to believe that I could have a future as a tennis player. Everyone at home played,

4. *Forehand* is a movement in which the tennis player hits the ball holding the racket with the palm facing forward. (N. E.)

and that contributed to my development, but it didn't take me long to dedicate myself to something else.

My sister played volleyball at the Fluminense club and, probably for convenience, our mother started taking me with her. The lessons took place twice a week in the afternoons, but I was soon nominated for a place on the club team.

The training days increased and, above all, the teacher changed. My second teacher was none other than Bené, a legendary volleyball coach who had worked with players like Bernard and Bernardinho, among other stars of the Brazilian national team at the time. He was very respected and strict. I once injured my little finger playing handball at school. As I couldn't miss training at all, I went to the club with my finger bandaged to explain what had happened and try to at least watch the group practice. Bené listened carefully to my explanation and asked me: "You hurt your little finger, right? And who said you use that finger to play volleyball?"

I tried to explain that my finger was throbbing and quite sore, and before I could finish the sentence, he handed me a 3-kilogram *medicine ball* and said: "Go to that wall and do a thousand touches with this ball. Then come back here and I'll give you another exercise".

He taught me, among many things, that it's always possible to do something, no matter what your situation, and that champions don't lose training, because it's irretrievable. Great lessons learned.

I played in two Rio championships for Fluminense, but our team was bad and we rarely won a game. Bené was always there, shouting at everyone as if it were the final of the championship. It was an interesting time and a lot of learning, but I didn't know anyone, my teammates weren't my friends, I was no longer at the Federal Club, and everything was discouraging me, just like volleyball itself.

Adolescence is definitely a difficult phase, with lots of changes, doubts, new paths and friendships. It's the time when we start to gain some freedom and, as parents aren't always around, it's impossible not to feel some degree of insecurity. We often make the wrong choices just to be included in that new group.

I had my friends from school, with whom I'd been studying since kindergarten. As a teenager, I started walking home alone or with some friends who lived in the same direction. We walked along the Ipanema promenade, a path that was almost always safe and definitely very beautiful.

My routine was always the same, and it started early in the morning with getting ready for school – and the first dispute of the day with my brothers to see who would sit in the front of the car with my father, who dropped us off at school, less than ten minutes from home, before heading off to work in the Bonsucesso neighborhood.

My father worked at Nestlé for over thirty years. His mornings were tense and, to make sure everyone woke up on time, he would start by calling us every five minutes. Finally, if nothing worked, a glass of iced water was infallible.

After school, I'd have lunch at home, watch the sports news on TV and, in the middle of the afternoon, go to my English course or another compulsory activity. Then I'd practice sports at the club until the evening, when my parents would also arrive. We'd all come home together and get on with the week.

CHAPTER 3

Jiu-Jitsu in my life

Every day my independence grew and, with it, my insecurity. I began to feel that it would be great to learn how to fight, and I had already been involved in several fights at school and at the club. Just the fact that I was more athletic and willing already guaranteed me some results, but I began to realize that this advantage wasn't true. It was time to try another sport – for the first time, fighting.

Karate was my first choice, as I used to watch Bruce Lee movies on television and thought it would be great to be able to fight like that. Leblon was home to one of the best academies in the country, Shotokan, run by master Hiroyasu Inoki, and that's where I enrolled. I would run along the beach for just over two kilometers, train and take the bus back. I did this three times a week – on the other days, I tried to apply what I had learned to my brother, which never worked.

I continued training for about six months until one day, watching the sports news, something caught my eye. Rei Zulu, a gigantic fighter from Maranhão who must have weighed 120 kilos of pure muscle, appeared on television saying more or less the following: "I challenge any fighter to a fight with no rules, but don't let any karateka come, because it'll be an 'ouch' to get in and an 'ouch' to get out"[5].

He was referring to the *kiai*, a cry of energy often used by karateka. That intrigued me. A few days later, a dark, thin young man with a very quiet voice accepted the challenge[6]. He calmly explained that the family he belonged to would never run away, and that he was ready to face anyone.

It was fascinating to think how a kid like that could beat a huge man like King Zulu, with more than two hundred vale tudo fights. That's how jiu-jitsu came onto my radar.

At school and at the club, I turned to my friends for more information while I tried to convince my mother to let me stop karate and enroll in jiu-jitsu. A friend, Pedro, had already practiced and told me he would do it again if I went with him. So we found an academy, originally Judo, near our school in Posto 6 in Copacabana. It wasn't that close to my house, but I agreed and we went there. The owner was Carlos de Tarso, who welcomed us very well and introduced us to Toninho, a super-sympathetic teacher in his fifties, who quickly offered us a lesson.

It was a very small place, in the basement of Galeria Alaska, a bohemian spot in Rio that wasn't very popular. We arrived at around 8pm and left at 8pm, so we weren't affected by the place. At the entrance, a small wooden table served as a reception desk. To the right was a changing room that could fit maybe four people at a time. To the left, a mat measuring about four meters by eight, with a single window at the end.

The first lessons were simply incredible; everything was logical and efficient. As the academy had few students, we received a lot of attention from the teacher, who grew fond of me as he saw that I was really dedicated and eager to learn.

---

5. Even though he was not a Jiu-Jitsu player, King Zulu repeated a challenge that was characteristic of the Gracie family at the beginning of the practice of the martial art in Brazil.

6. Later, I found out it was Rickson Gracie.

A few months into Jiu-Jitsu, my fights with my brother began to change: I no longer needed size or strength, because the technique I already possessed was enough to dominate him. I loved it, the feeling of power in dominating a brother three and a half years older. I never missed a training session and, when I had been in the gym for about six months, Fernando decided to train too. This was great because I had company to go back and forth with, as well as someone to practice with at home. At that time, Pedro reduced the frequency of his workouts.

My sister, Flavia, two years older than me, started dating Heleno, a very nice man who was the same age as our older brother and lived a block behind our house in Ipanema. He frequented the beach in the same place and was highly respected by the street gang. The reason? He was a blue belt in the Gracie academy. Heleno's jiu-jitsu was much better than ours and we trained together from time to time.

After about a year of practicing, jiu-jitsu was already my passion. I gave up all other sports and dedicated myself exclusively to it. Then we were informed that the academy would be closing down and our teacher recommended that we move to the mats of Pinduka, a Carlson Gracie star, at the end of Copacabana. Pedro followed this advice, but as it was too far away for me, we split up. I turned to Heleno and asked him to take me to train with him.

We agreed to go one evening to the gym in Rua Figueiredo Magalhães, in Copacabana. Originally, the place was shared between Carlson and Rolls, who alternated days of the week to train their students. When Rolls died, Carlos took over his share and the place was renamed Carlos Gracie Jr.

We went upstairs and, even though I hadn't planned to train straight away, I was quite nervous to see what it would be like. Heleno ran to the changing room to change while I sat watching the class. The mat was packed, and I remember the pairs doing technique while Carlinhos walked between them correcting the students.

There, I began to visualize what my days would be like and how I would get to Copacabana. The training was very different from what I was used to – as well as a lot of undergraduates, there was a different intensity to what we did at the other gym.

I really wanted to be a part of it. So, when I got back, I asked Heleno when I could start classes; he said he didn't think I should train at his gym, because it was too crowded and the training was for adults only. For him, it wouldn't be a good choice because I wouldn't get the attention I needed to develop.

I was disappointed, and I even thought it was him who didn't want me to train in the same place, but then I realized that it wasn't my destiny.

CHAPTER 4

Jacaré jiu-jitsu

A few days after visiting Carlos Gracie Jr. with Heleno, he told me about a gym that had opened in Ipanema near my house, where the teacher was a black belt – graduated by the legendary Rolls – called Romero Jacaré.

"A gym starting with a great teacher is the best possible setting for learning," he told me.

I was very excited. After all, it would be easier to convince my mother to let me train three blocks from my house than in Copacabana and, according to Heleno's arguments, I would be in great hands.

The gym offered a late afternoon slot that fit perfectly into my routine, as it was right after my English course on Tuesdays and Thursdays, and I could go straight to training.

When I arrived with my mother to check prices and schedules, I met Jacaré and my impression was the best possible. I was warmly welcomed and, when I mentioned that I had trained with Toninho for a year, I discovered that Toninho had also been Jacaré's first teacher, many years before, at the Gracie academy. An incredible coincidence.

With everything agreed, I started training under the tutelage of master Romero Jacaré Cavalcanti. In my initial class, I did the warm-up, the techniques of the day and, when it came to training, the teacher matched up the pairs. I trained very well with the students; even though I was only fourteen years old, I already had a good physical build and some technique.

I did well in the first and second, until Jacaré himself asked me to train with him. I don't remember that training session very well – perhaps because of the emotion – but, according to him, I got beaten up a lot. To this day, he says laughingly that he thought: "I don't think this kid is coming back".

I was extremely happy to be able to do jiu-jitsu and have a new home, and I finally understood that Heleno's recommendation had been very right – the place had a great atmosphere and Jacaré was a very attentive and dedicated teacher. The next day, I was back. That place transformed my life and shaped me as a man.

The academy, originally a Judo academy, was in the basement of a residential building at the beginning of Rua Visconde de Pirajá, in Ipanema. There were three rooms of around sixty square meters: the first was a mat, the second a gym, and the third a weight room.

The place didn't belong to Jacaré, who only had a few hours a week to teach jiu-jitsu. Divided by a pillar next to the only two small windows, there was a cramped changing room with an unheated shower. It didn't take long for the training sessions to start filling up and for Jacaré to get more times throughout the day. I attended whenever I could, and my skills improved rapidly.

Jacaré, at that time, trained with Rickson at the Gracie academy in Humaitá on Mondays, Wednesdays and Fridays at eleven o'clock in the morning. I loved hearing the stories that came in every day about the training sessions, the friendships, the Gracie family, the fights they took part in – it was all very cool and I realized that it was a world I wanted to be part of.

Championships weren't very common at the time and only happened occasionally. Anyway, when one of the most iconic stores in Rio de Janeiro announced that it was holding the first Jiu-Jitsu Company Cup, Jacaré asked who would like to fight at the gym. I immediately came forward. However, the minimum age was eighteen, and I had just turned fifteen – I couldn't even be a blue belt, since the minimum age is sixteen.

Even so, as I was already training with the adults, Jacaré agreed to take me to the selection camp at the Gracie academy. If I did well, we'd think about how to resolve the issue.

I arrived to compete in the sectional as an orange belt and, although I fought reasonably well, I lost the qualifier and missed out on the championship. I met Rickson, who was coordinating, organizing and refereeing some fights, and I remembered the image of the boy on television accepting the challenge of King Zulu, won by Gracie[7]. Now I was on the same mat, part of the same team, and he was extremely kind, even complimenting me on my performance.

I realized that I needed to train a lot more. If I couldn't even qualify, imagine if it was an official championship? I came back determined to dedicate myself even more to training and, even before I reached the minimum age, I received my blue belt from Master Jacaré.

The academy continued to grow a lot, and the group already had so many athletes that Gracie couldn't hold an internal selective. My master then decided that we would compete for the newly founded Jacaré Jiu-Jitsu, bringing together the students from Ipanema and Leblon, where he still taught on Tuesday and Thursday evenings.

The championship took place at the Military Club of Rio de Janeiro, in the Jardim Botânico neighborhood, and was financed by Vansport, a sporting goods store. We set up the team and, at the last minute, got a sponsor who offered a kimono for each athlete.

Back then, there were two types of kimono: the braided one – like the one we wear today – and the reinforced one – the

7. Rickson won with a rear naked choke, a technique that consists of strangling the opponent from behind.

one we got, which was plain, made of twill, much simpler and lighter. The kimono was horrible, but we had to wear it. After all, fighting in a first championship with sponsorship was unthinkable.

The event was divided into two weekends: the first was reserved for the qualifying rounds and the second for the semi-finals and finals.

I initially fought Adilson Lima, an athlete I faced several times afterwards and who became a great champion and jiu-jitsu teacher. I finished that fight with a triangle[8]. Then I waited for the winner of the bout between Manimal and Jessé, extremely strong athletes who lifted the gym in an electrifying fight.

As I watched, I thought about how aggressive they were, wondering how I would face one of them. Jacaré, who probably read my thoughts, pulled up next to me and commented: "How brutal! These guys will be no match for your technique. Anyone can come. Let's warm up for next time".

His aim was clearly to get me out of there so that I would stop watching that fight in which the competitors were killing each other, reaching the limits of the rules. Visually, it looked more like a brawl, with takedowns and pile-drives – a move now banned in championships, in which the athlete throws his opponent to the ground when inside his guard. The winner was Manimal, a famous student of Carlson's and a great grappler[9] and my next opponent.

When the fight started, I pulled on the closed guard[10] , swept[11] and mounted[12] , but stabilizing a strong competitor like Manimal isn't easy. At first, it was very difficult. He turned

8. The triangle consists of strangling your opponent with your legs.

9. Slang used to refer to fearsome fighters, who face any challenge, are resilient, focused.

10. It involves jumping with your legs around your opponent's waist.

11. Scraping is an inversion movement, when the athlete comes out of the bottom position using their legs.

12. The mount is the position of maximum dominance in jiu-jitsu, when the athlete stands on top with both knees on the ground, sitting on the opponent's chest.

his back and stood up, to which I immediately put the hooks[13] and became a backpack on his back.

Finally, I heard when someone outside tried to persuade him to throw himself backwards and fall on top of me, as he had done in the previous fight. Even when Manimal replied that he would never do that – because I was a kid and he had to beat me in technique – I thought it was wiser to get out of the backpack position.

I managed to steer the fight to a smooth victory, and received a great lesson from Manimal about sporting ethics and values: winning at any price is not the way to go.

I qualified for the semi-finals the following week, and I was still going to try for the absolute, a category with no weight limit. In my first fight, I suffered an attack on my arm[14] , which I defended although I wasn't able to undo the position. I was stuck for a few minutes until I heard Jacaré's instructions from the other side of the gym telling me to jump over to the left. It was the light I needed. Following his advice, I undid the position and got out of danger. There wasn't enough time to turn the match around, and I lost out on the advantage. I was satisfied with my performance on that first day of the championships, and happy because I had qualified for the semi-finals.

My opponent was set, a Gracie student, Carlos Eduardo. I don't remember if he also took part in the first internal selection, but I was confident, because I was already a completely different fighter at that point.

Our academy still had a strong link with his, as Jacaré and Malibu, a brown belt at the time and invited to help with classes, still attended. As well as having practiced with Rolls and Rickson, being a prepared fighter and a lot of fun, he trained a lot with our class. Malibu not only taught, but also

13. Hooks are a back takeover in which the feet are placed on the inside of the opponent's thighs.

14. An attack on the arm is an attempt at an *armbar*, a blow that has the power to end a fight.

gave us a real idea of the technical level we were reaching. So we agreed that it would be nice for me to go to a different training session, perhaps even at Gracie.

I don't remember whose idea it was, but the fact is that I was stopped by Rickson himself, who kindly explained that he couldn't allow it, as I would be facing a student from there. We were friends, but we represented different teams.

I heard about my opponent's qualities, what he was good at, what fights he had won so far and so on. This actually happened many times during my career.

People tend to deify their opponents, pay attention to comments that often add nothing. It's one thing to analyze a characteristic of your opponent objectively, it's another to project that they are better than they actually are.

I wasn't shaken at all and went into the fight with my strategy well defined. I passed the guard[15] , mounted and finished to qualify for my first championship final.

The final was against a Carlson veteran, Bráulio Carsalade. The fight was even and there were no points. When we got up and stood with the referee between us to announce the winner, we faced the three side judges. They would vote with flags: white in my favor, and green and yellow in favor of the opponent. Everyone had to raise them at the same time. The first two were divided, one for each of us. The third judge was Carlson himself – it was quite common at the time for teachers to help with the refereeing – who sealed my defeat with the green and yellow flag.

This was my first competition, and I came second in the adult category at just fifteen years old. I was happy with the result, but the most remarkable thing was attracting the attention of several friends from Jacaré, who came to praise my performance, express their support for the injustice of my

15. Passing the guard is a movement in which you pass your opponent's leg defense, reaching the control of the torso in an immobilization; it is worth three points in a competition.

defeat, encourage me and tell me that I had a great future. All those comments nurtured my desire to dedicate myself even more, and fed my certainty that I could be really good at jiu-jitsu.

It was time to get back to the gym and train.

CHAPTER 5

The first title

The year 1985 was coming to an end and, while I continued to progress on the mats, things weren't going so well at school. I was never one of the most studious students, but I always passed the year without too much difficulty.

In the first year of high school, classes had naturally become more rigid, but I only thought about training and had no time for other things. I gave up other sports, relegating them to the weekends when I practiced for pleasure, and jiu-jitsu became my priority - although that didn't free me from other obligations.

At the end of the year, I had a few retakes at school - nothing that had never happened before - and I remained confident that everything would work out. There would be fifteen days of tutoring and exams. Anyway, I failed Portuguese and Physics. The idea of delaying a year of my school life seemed terrifying and hit my family like a bombshell.

We analyzed the possibilities: continue at the same school and repeat the first year - which I thought was terrible - or change and do what they called dependency - in addition to the regular school year (second year), I would have classes in the two subjects I had failed, in the afternoon. My parents and I decided on the second option, because I wouldn't "lose the year". Of course, I also heard hours of lectures on the importance of being responsible, the value of opportunities, the need to sacrifice for important things, that life isn't just about desires, the responsibilities we need to fulfill, etc.

Although the end of the year was tumultuous, the vacations finally arrived and I experienced them differently. It wasn't just about not having fixed schedules and the freedom to do what I wanted, or even the lack of commitments and not being burdened by all the responsibilities imposed by my parents. It was a time to train even harder, to spend my days between the gym, exercising on the beach, eating healthy meals and everything else that is part of the jiu-jitsu lifestyle.

At the time, Jacaré was already using all the space for classes, and we started training from morning to night, from Monday to Friday. I asked him how he'd managed it, and he explained that he'd bought Alípio Amaral's and Zé Paulo's shares. From that moment on, we built the Jacaré jiu-jitsu house, another incentive for me to dedicate myself even more.

We renovated, changed the mats, painted the walls and thought about the logo we would use to represent our team. In the meantime, I trained all day and participated as much as I could. I kept a close eye on how Jacaré took care of the gym and the students, and made myself available to help him with whatever he needed. Due to his busy schedule, he had to stop teaching at Coelho, in Leblon. Some of his students then started training with us in Ipanema, further strengthening our team.

I had never trained as much as I did that summer. This new meaning of "vacation" was very good. I could see it when I went back to school and, with the routine of the gym re-established and the presence of the other fighters, my jiu-jitsu was already totally different. I made progress, and the students who had trained hard with me at the start of the vacation were no longer standing in front of me. It was a great feeling to see my efforts rewarded.

Jacaré used to tell us a fable by Aesop, an Ancient Greek author, about the ant and the cicada – the first worked during the summer while the other only sang. "Those who work hard in good times reap the rewards in difficult times," is the message we take from the story. I've felt it myself and I've learned more and more the value of effort and sacrifice for what we want.

The first championship of the year was announced, the Lightning Bolt Cup, a surf brand that took advantage of the rapport between the two disciplines and the growth of jiu-jitsu. We had a small team compared to traditional teams, basically made up of blue belts. After the qualifying rounds, four of our athletes went on to compete: Andrezinho, Alexandre Paiva, Marcelo Ribeiro and myself.

I reached the final of the middleweight category against Jessé Rodrigues, the same athlete who had fought that electrifying match against Manimal in my first tournament the year before. It was going to be very difficult and tough.

The fight started and I pulled closed guard, working my back techniques on the ground. After a few actions and exchanges of grips, I managed to get a tight triangle. My opponent resisted and I held on, applying as much pressure as I could. At one point, I put both hands on his head to create even more pressure for the choke. He stood up, lifting me completely off the ground and throwing me back with all his strength and weight. I absorbed the blow and squeezed even harder.

Jessé seemed to fall unconscious, and I thought the fight was over – his face was turning purple. Then I gave a little relief, and he quickly got up, bringing me along and throwing me back on the mat.

This opened the[16] lock that I had made with my legs, and removed the danger of the choke. There was very little to go and, after almost four minutes of unsuccessful squeezing, the judges gave me the win unanimously.

And that was my first jiu-jitsu title.

16. Position in which the legs are intertwined to apply the triangle with one foot positioned behind the other knee.

André won the bantamweight championship, with Marcelo in second place. Alexandre, who had lost at lightweight, won the absolute category in a great performance. Our result put Jacaré Jiu-Jitsu on the podium for the first time in fourth place, behind only the already established academies of the Gracie family. We were all very happy and proud.

Rickson fought a judoka called Marco André, a very tough fighter who had beaten other Gracie fighters. In the fight, Rickson pulled guard, attacked the triangle and armbar, which were defended. He then swept, passed the guard, mounted, took the back and choked – to the delight of the crowd.

One scene at the end really struck me: after the three taps that mark his opponent's defeat, Rickson got up with his hands full of blood and wiped them on the mat. Surely one of the choke attempts had cut his mouth, but it was a moment that showed who was really in charge in jiu-jitsu at the time.

Fighting in championships has always been a great learning experience. Firstly because of the experience, the emotional control, the difficulties overcome, among many other things, and because it was the only opportunity to see the great champions in action. Watching the fights of Rickson, Royler, Cassio Cardoso, Delariva and others was like having access to study material for months.

Then, on the Monday after the championship, everyone trained and analyzed the mistakes they had made, applying techniques that we had seen the higher-ups do. As always, it was time to dedicate ourselves even more.

The first time I saw Royler fight – I think it was his first black belt championship, and my first blue -, he applied an omoplata[17], which became known as the "fashion key" because it was a novelty I'd never seen myself. After the championship, we all went to the academy to study every sweep, every guard pass and everything else we had seen. That's how we evolved.

17. A blow that applies a shoulder lock to the opponent using one's own legs.

CHAPTER 6

Starting to teach

With the title, I became a bit more prominent in the gym and started helping Jacaré in as many classes as I could – and there were many. He would demonstrate the techniques on me, ask me to lead the warm-up and help the newcomers adapt to the class. I got a taste for explaining and trying to figure out how to be understood. I felt that the students appreciated my help.

One of them owned a pharmacy in Ipanema and used to train with us in the mornings. He really wanted his son to go to the gym, but the boy lived in Tijuca and couldn't get there. So he asked if I could give him private lessons. I replied that I was still a blue belt, and he insisted, showing his confidence in me: "I'm sure you'll teach very well".

I thanked him and went to talk to Jacaré, who didn't see any problem. I started teaching him on Saturdays at a gym in Tijuca, at 4pm. To do this, I would leave the house two hours earlier, take the bus – which was full because I was coming back from the beach – and it would take me at least another hour to get home. I loved teaching, and I started to get paid a lot for it.

The new school, however, changed my routine a lot. Although it advertised a lot for its special entrance exam classes, it didn't offer the best educations in the city. I soon realized that the large school system was much more impersonal than

I was used to. I knew almost no one and the teachers didn't even know who I was. What's more, my father didn't drive me anymore, which meant I had to get up earlier to take the bus.

One of the gym's main workouts took place in the morning, at 11 o'clock, which encouraged me to leave school early. As a result, I accumulated a significant number of absences. The more I disconnected from classes, the less I wanted to go. I started training in the morning and returning to the gym at four o'clock, staying until the evening.

The next day, I was always tired. I decided to adopt a strategy that ended up causing me serious problems: I would wake up early and say goodbye to my parents who were getting ready for work. Then I'd get a mattress from under my bed and go down to the party room, where I'd continue sleeping. When my father's car left the garage, I'd go back home, get my kimono and go training.

One day, he asked the doorman if I'd been out for a long time, and the clerk replied that he hadn't seen me and that I usually went out later. It wasn't long before I was found sleeping in the party room. The feeling of being caught cheating and disappointing my father was horrible, but I argued that I was dedicating myself to sport and that school was getting in the way - obviously to no avail.

He told me that his house was no place for a liar; that if I was capable of cheating at home, I would do the same anywhere - including in sport. He told me that I needed to be responsible for my attitudes and commitments. He explained that I had to build an image of reliability and honor. These were teachings that I have carried with me throughout my life.

The next day, we went to the school to talk to the principal. When we arrived, the principal, who was also a chemistry teacher - a subject I had missed most of - greeted me with a "nice to meet you" and a chuckle that set the tone for what was to come.

When my father asked about my real situation at school, we heard: “Mathematically, he’s failed for absences”. Then the teacher suggested a deal. “It’s simple, young man,” he said. “You’ll stay for all the summer retakes. If you manage to pass all eleven subjects, I’ll cancel your absences and you’ll pass the year”.

I went for it, because it was my chance to get out of that vexatious situation and make up for my mistake. I studied everything I hadn’t even seen all year, and I managed to pass.

△

CHAPTER 7

No Kimono

Our academy continued to grow. Me, Alexandre and Marcelo Ribeiro received our purple belts. Until I was sixteen, I had never done anything with the quality and determination with which I did jiu-jitsu – and not just training, but helping Jacaré in any way I could. I'd go to the bank to make deposits, check attendance sheets, help with classes, etc.

Our team now had reinforcements. In addition to my brother Fernando, we also had Traven, Mauricio, Peck, Telo and others. We were a respected group. We fought hard in every tournament and competition that came our way.

I remember a special event, the 3rd Jiu-Jitsu Company Cup, the most coveted championship at the time. We took the entries to Gracie, where the draw would be made and the brackets set up, and when we got there with Jacaré, we found all the teachers gathered – the Gracie academies and their respective representatives, Carlson, Rickson and Carlinhos, as well as other smaller associations like ours.

The conversations began about who would be in whose category and how the draw would be made. Watching those debates taught me a lot about how to put together the best team possible.

In one of his discussions with Rickson, Master Carlson told him to stop arguing over things: "If you want, you can put all your blue belts up against mine. In blue, I only care about Jacaré's students".

No compliment could be more important than Carlson's comment. Jacaré was a little miffed, but certainly full of pride.

The Company Cup was a big event at the Fluminense Club gymnasium, where years before I had competed in the Rio volleyball championships. Unlike then, with jiu-jitsu my victory only depended on me. I fought four times in the middleweight category, won and was champion.

I faced Jean Jacques Machado in the absolute, in a tough fight that I lost by split decision. On the day of the draw, I remember Rickson commenting that only a black belt could beat Jean Jaques, because he was at a much higher level than the average purple belt. As I also considered myself above average, I wasn't intimidated. In the end, we had a nice, even fight.

A few weeks later, the Company launched an event T-shirt with the names of all the champions – and I was there. "Purple belt champion: Fabio Gurgel".

This phase was short, but very intense. I only spent a year and a half there, but I realized that I could be a good jiu-jitsu teacher and I began to fall in love with the process of seeing the effect of what I taught on other people. I couldn't explain why, and I didn't even think about it much, but teaching became as important to me as fighting.

Jacaré always provided as many opportunities as he could for us to help him and, little by little, the students began to trust me and enjoy the lessons. I could do it all day. I trained with whoever I wanted, I was always available and my kimono was always clean, attitudes that increased Jacaré's trust in me.

Then he decided to travel to Indonesia and asked if I could teach for a fortnight. It was the first time I had responsibility for the class in my hands. The weeks went by and the only thing that arrived was a postcard saying that everything was fine, and that he would stay a little longer if it was all right with me. I went on for fifty days and, when Jacaré returned, he found everything exactly as he had left it, as well as happy students and me even more sure of what I was going to do for a living.

Jiu-jitsu was already my profession, and I couldn't have had a more vibrant youth.

As the championships became more competitive, my training also intensified. The Gracie students originally trained three times a week. When Carlos Júnior moved to Barra, Carlson's students started training every day.

As Jacaré was also a physical education teacher and triathlete – he had just completed the *Ironman* in Hawaii – he guided our preparation, taking us to another level. Instead of three workouts a week, we did more than ten between jiu-jitsu and conditioning.

Healthy eating, an important part of the Gracie family culture, has been fully incorporated by Jacaré and consequently by us. The diet is based on the chemical compatibility of food and, the story goes, was developed by master Carlos Gracie. Prioritizing a long and healthy life, it combines lots of fruit and cottage cheese.

We took turns – me, my brother, Gigi and Jacaré – to go to CEASA every week to buy everything in bulk: boxes of apples, papaya, oranges, guavas. The fridge in my house had to accommodate all of this plus an average of 48 glasses of cottage cheese every month, apart from the family's needs – which obviously didn't accommodate our diet. I followed this diet for years, sometimes radically, and I still follow many of the principles I learned back then.

Awareness of the importance of what we eat came into my life at a time when we are usually exposed to a lot of junk food. Even though they seem harmless to young people, they create a bad habit and jeopardize our health forever.

Example is undoubtedly a determining factor in our choices, and I have always been inspired by Jacare and his lifestyle. Food became a fundamental part of my routine, and certainly one of the most valuable lessons that universe taught me.

Although I was still very young, jiu-jitsu became a source of self-esteem for me. Realizing the admiration and respect I caused in others, feeling the power of a technique that, in a way, placed me above people – not only in combat, but also in other matters such as health, discipline, problem solving, etc. -made me feel satisfied with myself.

I dedicated myself to becoming better and to continuing to evolve, but one doubt remained in my mind: would I really have the advantage in a real fight that people imagined? I'd never tried it – apart from a few sporadic fights at school and with my brother as a child, all without much consequence. All my experience came from training, not from a real fight.

I've always heard countless stories coming from all sides, and I've come to understand that fighting should never be the goal, nor the incentive. However, our honor cannot be ignored. Where we draw the line on what we accept or don't accept as a blemish on our name is quite individual, and I would venture to say even flexible – it depends on various issues.

I needed to be prepared. So I became interested in vale-tudo techniques, and training without a kimono – in which punches and kicks were accepted – became a constant after school.

I usually practiced with Traven, my great partner at the time, and we started taking private lessons with master Reyson Gracie, affectionately called master Filhinho by Jacaré – and later by all of us. He would come to the gym in the afternoons and teach us the basics, as well as a few tricks. I learned very important lessons, such as the importance of the pisão[18] combined with the *jab*[19].

---

18. A kicking technique that aims to maintain distance from the other.
19. In boxing, it is a preparatory punch thrown with the front hand.

The master explained that if you land a good knee strike on your opponent and he moves his leg back to avoid the blow, he will be forced to project his face forward, which is where your *jab* will find him. On the other hand, if you don't, hitting the jab will put you at the perfect distance to grab him.

Master Reyson is currently the patriarch of the Gracie family.

CHAPTER 8

Jiu-jitsu in practice

One afternoon on Ipanema beach, the line I had drawn to guarantee my honor was crossed for the first time. I was playing in a sand soccer championship, in a very even game. Telo and Traven, my gym buddies, were on my team. The promenade was packed and there were fans cheering on both sides at every turn. I was playing in midfield and, when the opposing team's star player received the ball, I was the first to mark him. I noticed the ball going over my head – the famous "sheet", a beautiful dribble that would have been clean if I hadn't used my jiu-jitsu. Realizing that I couldn't avoid the shot, I wrapped my arms around my opponent's waist. He tried to get out of my grip and I applied a hip drop. It was a clear foul and I received a very well-deserved yellow card. We both laughed, and he prepared to take the penalty. Then a fan who was standing on the sidewalk started shouting: "Hey, asshole, you're going to sleep in the cold tonight, huh?"

I didn't pay any attention, and he shouted back. Then I looked at him and asked if he was talking to me. He agreed, repeating the provocation.

The penalty was called and the game went ahead, but I couldn't stop thinking about that insult. Every time I looked at the sidewalk, there he was staring at me and mocking me. I commented to Traven and Telo during the game that I would question the fan at the end. They both agreed that he was very loose, as well as being known in the area as a bully. His name was Mario.

We won the game and, after the final whistle, we went behind the goal to return the uniforms. The fan taunting me was no longer on the sidewalk, but on the other side of the field playing goal with some friends. I called out to Telo and Traven so they wouldn't let anyone get in the way or separate us. Then I approached him and asked: "Weren't you the one who wanted to talk to me?".

He started to say yes, but I interrupted him with a slap to the face with my right hand, followed by a waistlock[20] and a fall. Falling in the sand is even more comfortable than on the mat, and he fell on his ass, I landed the first punch on the side of his face. My opponent immediately turned his back to protect himself, but these instinctive reactions are so common and predictable that my next move was automatic: I slipped a choke from behind and began to squeeze until Telo calmly told me that I could let go because my opponent had passed out. In just over twenty seconds, the fight was over and I felt a sense of dishonor washed away. I left immediately, after all, I had heard from older fighters that you shouldn't stay at the scene of a fight, because the chance of retaliation was too great. Later, I heard that the boy was fine, had woken up without any problems and from then on his nickname was *Mario Soninho.*

***

Our gym, as well as becoming a benchmark for the work carried out by the master, was undoubtedly the best located in Rio de Janeiro, in the heart of Ipanema, on the famous

20. A *clinch* technique in which the opponent is hugged under the arms.

Visconde de Pirajá street. We received countless visitors, such as Jacaré's friends who used to drop by to have a "little workout" with Jessé's boys, the nickname by which Jacaré is called by his closest friends. Almost all the big names in the Gracie academy at the time visited our little mat.

After some time at purple belt, training began to get more intense and very few fighters left without being "squeezed" by our group. Alexandre "Gigi" Paiva had already reached an impressive level and was the terror of the famous visitors. These moments were undoubtedly fundamental to our evolution.

People who did other martial arts also used to show up. I specifically remember three boys who trained in *Taekwondo*. I don't know what their intention was, but Jacaré convinced them to test their style against ours. The rule was simple: they could kick, punch and use any blow they wanted. It was up to us just to block and take them down, dominating them on the ground. Although it doesn't seem very fair, that's how we dealt with other fights, so confident were we in our technical superiority, and this episode proved how easy it was to grab and take down someone who didn't know jiu-jitsu.

As the visits dwindled, Gigi and I talked it over and came to the conclusion that it would be great if we could train with Rickson too. After all, he was our idol and our master's teacher. We'd have a multitude of training sessions, and we'd certainly be closer to the source – at least that's what we thought at the time. So we were very well received by Rickson at Gracie, and we explained our intentions. Very kindly, he said: "It would be great to have two champions with your talent here at the academy. However, for that to happen, it's only natural that you leave Jacaré's academy".

I felt a pang of shame. Although it was obvious that this would be the condition, we hadn't thought about it. We replied that it wasn't a possibility. With a smile and a hug, he said as we said goodbye: "You've made the best choice".

CHAPTER 9

Total dedication

After I finished the third year of high school with some difficulty, it was time for the university entrance exams and not going to university was out of the question. I chose what seemed most appropriate for the career I had decided to pursue: physical education. At the time, there were only two public options in Rio de Janeiro, the Federal and State Universities, and one private, Gama Filho, where Jacaré had studied. I took the exams and passed into the second semester of the latter, so I would have another six months off with 100% free time to train. Nothing was more exciting for me, and even my parents seemed satisfied.

I was able to dedicate myself to what was really important to me. Training intensified. In the morning, I'd go to the gym; afterwards, I'd do some preparation on the beach, do some running on the ramp in Arpoador square or on the soft sand, swim around the Pedra, etc. Finally, I would enjoy the water, have lunch and go back to Jacaré, where I would teach until ten o'clock.

I started thinking about the improvements we could make for the students. I had always heard that Gracie had two days a week closed for private lessons. So I started encouraging Jacaré to offer this product, although he never really liked the idea. On the other hand, I believed that there would be a good demand at times when the space was empty.

Malibu, our main instructor, had just started teaching at Reyson Gracie and invited me to meet and talk to the master. It was a great experience, although the business model of this academy was very different from ours. It only offered semi-private and private classes, and the entire program was written on the wall for the students to follow, which made the teacher's job a lot easier – a curriculum to follow.

I thought it was a great idea and took it to Jacaré. We implemented it in our academy. We bought yellow cards and Gigi – who had the best handwriting – wrote the 36 lessons in what the master thought was the most appropriate style. We stuck them up on the wall, arousing the students' curiosity about all the techniques. We then explained that this was the program for private lessons, and the number of applicants began to increase.

The person who worked very well with them was a fellow Gracie who started training with us in the mornings, Sylvio Behring. Extremely technical and very attentive, he taught us a lot. We formed a great relationship and he allowed me to attend his morning classes at Corpo 4, near our school. I would get there at seven o'clock and sit in the corner of the mat watching him conduct his classes. With one student after another, and a style very much focused on self-defense, it was dynamic and fun, showing efficiency in teaching the art for an individual class. I was delighted and learned a lot. Gradually, he started to put me in as a helper and that was another rich period for me on my journey to becoming a good teacher.

During this time, championships continued to take place. The ritual was always the same: we'd receive the notice in the mail with the forms to fill in the names, separated by weight and belt, we'd try to convince as many students as possible to fight, and we'd take the list of those confirmed to the organizational meeting, which most of the time took place at Gracie do Humaitá. There, we would compare our list with those of the other teams. Then we made the draw, which usually took place the week of the championship, starting with blue belts up to black belts.

Jacaré didn't put my name in my category at the time, purple belt middleweight, and announced that I would be fighting in brown. I was very excited about the challenge, and I made my debut in this belt at the Rolls Gracie Cup. I was champion at my weight and in the absolute, putting on some great fights.

This championship took place at Clube Municipal, in the Tijuca neighborhood, where I had never fought until then. In that same gym, months earlier, there had been an emblematic event in the history of jiu-jitsu: a tournament exclusively for brown and black belts sponsored by Cantão, a clothing store that rivaled Company and which, for the first time, supported the martial art. As I was still purple, I didn't fight, but Jacaré was invited to be the referee for the event and Gigi and I were the assistants, which put us in a very good position to watch the fights.

In one of the most eagerly awaited finals of the event, between Royler Gracie and Ricardo De La Riva, Jacaré took the side flag – as a judge, he would only decide the fight in the event of a draw. Everything went as expected, a very tough and evenly matched fight. At the end of the ten minutes, we still didn't have a winner.

The central judge asked the flags to raise the color of their vote, and Jacaré hesitated. The other two judges chose different fighters and tension was in the air. For a few seconds, everyone felt the weight on Jacaré's shoulders. He had raised the flag in favor of De La Riva, i.e. Carlson's academy, against the Gracie academy of which he was a member.

Although he acted firmly and fairly in his assessment of the performances, this displeased the family and, the very next week, the climate was not good for Jacaré in the gym and with Royler himself.

For us, the result of this absence was Jacaré's full dedication to our team, and the morning training sessions became the main ones for the competition team, with our master leading us every day. The group's evolution has been brutal.

Another championship took place and this time I faced a student of Carlson's with whom I'd never fought before. As no one scored, I won on the judges' decision. However, I didn't do anything to be proud of in the fight. I didn't take any risks, I fought more afraid of losing than wanting to win, and I was only able to neutralize my opponent's actions. As I became champion, I was satisfied.

On the Monday after the championships, as usual, I went to train and got my medal – they were all hanging on the wall in the reception area. I got on the mat and began to receive congratulations on yet another title.

Even though I was happy with the win, when I went to talk to Jacaré, he asked me if I was happy with the performance in the fight the day before. He explained that I shouldn't celebrate a fight in which I didn't fight effectively, in which I didn't do anything and that sometimes it was better to lose fighting than to win like that.

I think it was one of the biggest and best criticisms the master ever gave me. He was absolutely right. I was aware that I had performed badly and yet I embraced the vanity of patting myself on the back instead of concentrating on how to do better.

We can't always be good or win, but we have an obligation to be true to ourselves.

My life was totally immersed in that world, although I still played soccer sporadically in some tournaments organized by the Federal Club. There, I had lots of friends of all ages, including my brother's class – three years my senior. They all knew that I practiced Jiu-Jitsu and some asked me to teach them. I suggested they go to Jacaré in Ipanema. However, they wanted to train at the club, where they already went and had autonomy to come and go.

We then approached the club's sports coordinator, who liked the idea. I asked Jacaré if he'd like to take over the training sessions, but he told me to do it myself, as I had enough experience. He also made himself available to help me with whatever I needed.

Within a few weeks, at the age of eighteen and with a brown belt, I was instructing six students in one room at the club. Before long, I had over a hundred and started earning money. I gave private lessons in the morning and group classes in the afternoon. In the evenings, I would run to Ipanema to train at Jacaré's gym.

Everything was falling into place between work and training, and I felt fulfilled. As an official teacher, I took on a great responsibility and began to dedicate myself to it. However, with college starting in the second semester, private classes in the morning would no longer be possible – Gama Filho University was located in the neighborhood of Piedade, in the suburbs of Rio.

Life as a teacher gradually changed me. I wanted to give the best lessons, make the students learn everything about jiu-jitsu, pass on the stories I had heard since I was a boy on the mats, train with them, influence them to adopt healthy habits and everything that would bring out their best.

I tried to feed my courage through challenging training and competitions. Before long, I was leading one of the best blue belt teams in the city.

I wasn't able to follow Sylvio Behring's private lessons, but our very close relationship led me to his brother, Marcelo, whom I had already seen fight a few times and who was Rickson's best pupil. He had moved to São Paulo, but traveled to Rio de Janeiro sporadically.

For an entire weekend, the Behring family organized a jiu-jitsu seminar in São Paulo. There were two sessions on Saturday and two on Sunday, a very rich experience. As well as the opportunity to learn various techniques, I got close to Marcelo and we began a friendship that has had an impact on my life. We often trained for days on end. His technique was refined and his creativity and *timing* very different. Although he showed the efficiency of sport jiu-jitsu, his passion was always for vale-tudo techniques.

After growing a lot with Reyson Gracie while still a purple belt, I experienced a new understanding of fighting with Marcelo. Our training sessions were very fruitful and fun, especially because he was an artist who taught both on and off the mat.

We were very different: he lived for the moment, while I planted for the future; he was impulsive, I was more reflective; he was fearless, I was more cautious; he was outgoing, I was more shy; he was more talented, I was more disciplined; he was more loving, I was more closed off. It was these differences that made us complete and our friendship was built up in a very solid way. Marcelo was fundamental in shaping me as a fighter.

But I was a long way behind him technically. Once, we trained for about thirty or forty minutes on the mats at the Federal Club. We started with the kimono and then applied vale-tudo techniques, where each slap to the face was worth a point. The score was thirty to ten for him.

I had the privilege of living with Marcelo for more than four years, experiencing incredible moments and absorbing the way in which one of jiu-jitsu's most brilliant practitioners saw the art. I was also a friend, a student, a confidant, I lived with his family, and to this day I can see how important he was in connecting people from different tribes.

Thinking of Marcelo always brings me the image of his generous laugh and, of course, an immense nostalgia for this great influencer in my history.

CHAPTER 10

Off the mat

In the second semester of 1989, I started a new routine when I began my physical education course. I would leave at six o'clock to take the train to Piedade and return at lunchtime for classes and training. Not that I liked the idea of swapping jiu-jitsu for college, but I understood the need to keep studying. Traven was in the same class, and that was certainly an incentive.

In the very first week, we started to hear that the freshman class was going to be hazed by the seniors. I remember thinking: "I don't think that's going to happen". At the time, I exchanged a look with Traven and we decided that, in our class, that prank wouldn't happen – at least not without a lot of fighting. So we offered the class protection, giving them the option of participating or not.

As we were already relatively well-known fighters, when the veterans came into our room with a threatening tone and ready to start playing humiliating and cowardly games, we stood up and explained that we wouldn't be taking part, and if anyone wanted to, they should raise their hand. No one spoke up and, for a few seconds, they didn't know what to do. We continued to stand looking at the group that had invaded our room and, little by little, they looked at each other, shook their heads and left muttering that we didn't know how to play. Our class was saved and we got through the hazing unscathed.

The college gave me the opportunity to train in Judo, providing a large mat – especially when compared to the one we used to train on in Ipanema – and classes in the sport. I joined the team and had the opportunity to compete in some tournaments, taking advantage of my jiu-jitsu experience – as I fought from white to green, I won the tournaments without much difficulty. When I wasn't training, I was doing physical training, swimming and anything else that would keep me going.

I finished 1989 as the best brown belt elected by the Liga Niteroiense de Jiu-Jitsu (LNJJ), the federation involved in most of the championships at the time. I lost very few fights, one of them to a Carlson athlete who would become the greatest opponent in my jiu-jitsu career, Amaury Bitetti.

On vacation, all we could think about was how to increase our training time. We knew that every break threatened our focus. So when I traveled with my family, I always took my kimono and "hunted" for a gym to train at. When I was with other fighters and friends, which was increasingly common, we would train and do physical preparation.

Jiu-Jitsu wasn't just a sport: it naturally became our way of life.

We were always together and, in programs outside the academy, we explored Rio de Janeiro. Every day we chose a place to practice. It wasn't unusual for us to bring in new followers, people who wanted to join the group.

Although everyone was welcome, they usually suffered and didn't return. What's more, they were "victims" of the Jacare who always loved to swim and go around Pedra do Arpoador, the source of many stories of drowning. For those who have never tried it, it seems easy. But the sea is rough at that point and practice suggests that the swimmer moves away from shore. As Jacaré was the champion of the course, we either followed him and swam away from the shore – which wasn't comfortable for me – or we suffered near the rock and almost drowned. In the end, everything was a competition:

who arrived first, in how much time, who almost drowned and who would be the target of comments and jokes. Fortunately, the worst never happened.

Competition was encouraged at every turn and reached its peak in everyday training.

Jacaré always had one characteristic as a teacher, and I particularly consider it to be one of his best qualities: pairing up the pairs, i.e. which student is going to train with whom. This helped us develop and kept us protected – it's what we know today as the *flow zone*. It's challenging, but possible, and really a difficult science to execute so masterfully.

Jacaré had another characteristic that wasn't so "programmed", but which helped us a lot: he was terrible at time management. We would train in heavy *rounds*, facing difficult teammates, and it often felt like the minutes were ticking away. No one wanted to be the first to ask, as it would show weakness and fatigue to their opponent. But, anyway, there was always someone who couldn't take it any longer and drew his attention to the count. Jacaré, most of the time totally distracted from enjoying the fights, would look at the clock and mark the end. We'd all laugh, and he'd say that "the time has just passed" – even if it had already expired many minutes ago.

In short, these moments of distraction ended up preparing us for the struggles and unpredictability of life. After all, how do we react when the boundaries we've set ourselves don't align with reality?

Championships were always just one aspect of our school, while the development of virtues was the mainstay.

Our group continued to grow and the academy, although very small by today's standards, already had many students, all of whom were encouraged to compete.

There was a sticker pinned up on our notice board at the time: "A tear for defeat is better than shame for not fighting". Every time a student tried to justify their decision not to compete, Jacaré would use this quote, which soon became a mantra within the school and made us an increasingly competitive team.

More than a team, we were a family, fighting for each other and feeling proud to represent our master. We all experienced the feeling of belonging to something bigger and far beyond the simple desire to win individually.

Jacaré's encouragement, above all, made me see challenges as something very natural to face. Every time we face a dispute, even an individual one, we tap into one of the fears of human beings: public humiliation.

Thoughts project possibilities, the mind imagines and suffers in anticipation of what may or may not be a defeat, while at the same time it is euphoric when it glimpses victory, the goal achieved. However, these are all just imaginary issues, which cause us a great deal of anxiety that is not very beneficial.

Seneca, one of the main Stoic philosophers, wrote in *The Shortness of Life* that we suffer 95% of the time from things that will never happen, because we torment ourselves in advance with our ability to imagine the future. The remedy for this is to concentrate on the present and what can be done at that very moment. We are the only living beings with the ability to understand the timeline, study the past and think about tomorrow. It is undoubtedly very tempting, and therefore difficult, to control this impulse. That's the whole source of the anxiety we experience and which causes so many problems for millions of people.

Competing and dealing with expectations helped me a lot. When I signed up for a championship, I had the desire to be champion, to show my technique in public, to represent my team, but I also experienced the fear of failing, of losing, of disappointing my master and my teammates. I've experienced all these feelings at different times in my career. I've fought very well and been champion, I've fought badly and been champion, I've disappointed my teammates and master, I've been hurt by the referees, I've won favored by them and so on.

The fact is that being on the battlefield makes us realize that, in every scenario, we become better. We exercise the virtue of courage by facing the fear of failure; we learn that when the positive result doesn't come, it sends a package of knowledge necessary for our development.

By constantly exposing ourselves to the challenge, that initially uncomfortable place becomes totally different, and even desirable, because that's where your development lies. Nothing is more motivating than becoming better than before. Being brought up in an environment where people value risk, admire competition and praise the champion certainly makes a difference.

***

The trigger for one of the most important moments in my career came on a Friday, when Traven and I arranged to train in Barra da Tijuca, at Carlos Gracie Jr.'s gym, with Jean Jacques Machado and Renzo Gracie.

When we arrived, they weren't there. Crolin Gracie welcomed us and told us that the next day Rickson would be facing an old Luta Livre opponent, Hugo, who had slandered him. He asked us not to talk to anyone, only Jacaré.

We were very excited, because we would be on a mission reserved for very few – only those close to the top of the family. We agreed to go together to Carlinhos' gym, where everyone would meet, and I hardly slept that night.

We arrived around ten o'clock, and Rickson, as well as several family members and some of the closest students, had already arrived. He explained that he was packing his bags for the USA, but wouldn't leave without someone talking about him without consequence.

We were all gathered at the gym waiting for the opponent and his gang to arrive on the scene. Ralph and Ryan Gracie were still kids, so they were going back and forth from the beach with the information.

As the weather was ugly – dull and sunless – there was uncertainty as to whether the fight would actually take place. Master Robson Gracie then asked: "Who organized this? Such a lack of planning isn't possible! An event of this magnitude in the open? Why didn't you talk to me before?"

Everyone laughed, but we continued to wait. The gym was full and someone gave us the idea of taking advantage of the time. It didn't take long for the mats to host one of the best workouts I've ever witnessed.

I started practicing with Carlos "Soneca" Machado and, when I finished, Rickson called me over. I had only faced him once before, when I was still a purple belt, but as we knelt facing each other and touched hands, a shout came from the door announcing the arrival of the other fighter on the beach.

Rickson said that he was going to walk along the promenade towards Hugo, and that he only wanted Rilion and Renzo by his side. All the others should arrive first and position themselves so that as soon as the fight started, they would close the circle and not let anyone separate.

The plan went exactly to plan. We monitored Rickson's arrival until he slapped Hugo in the face, and we ran to close the circle.

The fight started and Rickson got off balance, falling under at first. But he recovered quickly, getting back to his feet. The two exchanged a few punches without much efficiency and went to the ground again, this time with Gracie on top.

The tension in the circle grew with Hugo's friends wanting to see what was going on, but our group prevented them from entering the circle. A few moments later, Rickson was mounted, landing good blows to the face of his opponent, who surrendered. The code of honor of fights applies to these moments too and, in a clean fight, a withdrawal must be respected immediately.

When we got into the water, another fight broke out. This time, it was a quick clash between Renzo Gracie and Marcelo Mendes, who disagreed while still in the circle. There wasn't even time for people to separate them.

We all left, but the rivalry didn't end there. Other chapters of this story were still being written.

CHAPTER 11

The black belt

The martial arts taught from the beginning of the 20th century had the wisdom to create a symbolism to translate the student's journey, and the vast majority of people who start practicing have the goal – or even the dream – of becoming a black belt.

The white belt is the beginning, the starting point for absorbing new knowledge. The apprentice progresses along a road with different levels until they reach mastery and mastery not only of technique, but also of moral codes and emotional control.

The beginning was no different for me. I often wondered how it would feel to be a black belt. I admired the people who had made it, watched how they behaved, how they trained and often tried to copy them.

As I progressed, I realized that there are levels within this rank and, although the dream was very much alive inside me, I understood that the goal shouldn't be simply to achieve the belt, however symbolic that might be. I needed to evolve. That was the most important thing. The black belt would be an obvious consequence of my journey, and I couldn't control when or how I would receive it.

There was no ritual at the time – Jacaré had never graduated anyone to this level – and no minimum or maximum time in each belt. The change was, as it still is, the sole decision of the teacher, and it's not for anyone to dispute it – or even ask about it.

I stopped worrying and got on with my training and classes. One afternoon, as I was getting ready to train, the intercom rang: Reyson Gracie was waiting for me at the gate. I didn't understand; Master Filhinho had never been to my house before. I grabbed my kimono and went downstairs. Surprised to see him, I asked if anything had happened, and he told me he'd only gone to make sure I was going to train that day.

It was all very strange, especially because I was never absent and because he didn't go to Jacaré that often. We walked together to the gym, which was packed. At the time, I didn't even imagine that the mass presence of the students was planned or had anything special to do with it. But on that October 23, 1989, Jacaré insisted on everyone being present because he was graduating his first black belt fighter. At nineteen, with six years of jiu-jitsu under my belt, I couldn't have been prouder to be that student.

The ceremony was quick. The master spoke a few words about the importance of the moment, emphasizing my dedication and preparation for the challenges that lay ahead. We took lots of photos and I immediately went to wear my belt in the best way: training.

I felt very happy about the achievement, and even more excited about the world that was opening up in front of me. I would have the opportunity to compete with the biggest names in the sport, people would see me differently, and I could win over more students. I couldn't wait to experience it all.

***

There are two types of learning in any transition.

The first is that you haven't become drastically better than you were the day before because you have a new position. So you need to remain humble and with the same thirst for knowledge.

The second is that if you were one of the best at your previous stage, now you've been thrown to the back of the queue. After being voted the best brown of the year, I moved to the bottom of the black ranking. A long staircase had to be climbed to reach the top. Graduation was, like the previous ones, a new beginning, a new phase in my career. Never the end.

For a beginner, a black belt can be the end point, the culmination of their journey. But as we train, we discover that life is an eternal journey, a constant learning process and a permanent quest for improvement.

I often define jiu-jitsu as an activity in which you will never be good enough. Having the conviction that we don't know everything and that we need to continue dedicating ourselves to evolution with an open *mind* is what we call the "white belt *mindset*".

The black belt is undoubtedly a *milestone*, an important symbol that celebrates years of dedication and study, it represents knowledge and sacrifice, but it's not the end of the line.

It took six years to get to black belt and then thirty-one years between training and fighting, teaching and experiences. "When did I learn the most?" The answer is obvious. I was exposed to many more challenges after reaching black belt, which taught me much more than in the initial years. In particular, I learned not to bet all my chips and thoughts on one goal.

At this point, the reader may be confused, perhaps even wondering if they shouldn't "focus on an objective to achieve the result".

There are some books that argue that this is the case, and perhaps the best known is Malcolm Gladwell's *Outliers*. In it, the author defends the theory of ten thousand hours dedicated to becoming exceptional at any activity. He's not entirely wrong. I believe that we do need to dedicate ourselves even more than that.

The point is that we can't forget that we live in a more plural world, I believe, where our needs won't be met just because we're good at one thing; we need more knowledge.

In his book *Range: Why Generalists Triumph in a Specialized World*, author David Epstein challenges Gladwell's theory and shows the importance of having varied knowledge in order to become better at your core business.

Throughout my career intensely dedicated to jiu-jitsu, I was able to see the benefit of having practiced team sports, especially for my career as a teacher.

Reading has given me the knowledge to create better analogies to explain the techniques to my students, and so on.

Focusing on just one thing leads us down dangerous paths. We may simply miss the target. When we only have one desire, we usually aim high, setting a goal that makes us exceptional, such as achieving something difficult and relevant, being in a prominent place that many people want, getting into a competitive university or even becoming a world jiu-jitsu champion. When a dream doesn't come true despite years of dedication to this goal, we feel disappointed, discouraged and often frustrated. These anxieties can accompany us for many years and compromise our self-esteem – and, why not say it, make it difficult for us to succeed in life?

Let's look at an example. A certain elite swimmer competed for years and dedicated himself to the maximum for a few Olympic cycles. It was obviously many hours a day, many days a week, many weeks a year, all dedicated to one goal: the Olympic gold medal. However, this athlete competed against another, Michael Phelps, the greatest medal record holder in the history of swimming to date. Every time our fictional swimmer reached the final, he lost, sometimes by hundredths of a second.

Is he a failure? The answer is "it depends". If the Olympic gold medal was his only goal, then yes, he failed.

However, if his energy was dedicated to evolving every day of his training to reach his best version, and he created this habit for everything he set out to do, the answer is undoubtedly no. This swimmer developed to the best of his abilities, learned to deal with defeat, overcame his own limits and continued to dedicate himself even after setbacks. He is certainly much more capable and prepared for any challenge than most.

Results are not always a sign of excellence.

On the other hand, if we achieve our "unique goal" after years of dedicated training, if we win our "Olympic medal", we will be consumed by a moment of great joy and satisfaction, a sense of accomplishment. We will prove to everyone, and to ourselves, that we are capable, that all the effort was worth it. We have won, we will celebrate and we will be celebrated.

However, this euphoria is short-lived – it will last a few weeks, and maybe even less. Then those who celebrated us will go on to look after their own interests, and our lives will return to normal. The goal has been achieved, and motivation has naturally waned. We'll need a new goal, since we've already achieved that one.

Countless champions fall victim to this, because they don't understand that a certain result can't be the only goal, but just one step in the journey of building their legacy. When we see it this way, the euphoria of winning a medal won't discourage us.

Regardless of whether the result is positive or negative, I always work towards progress. Sooner or later, I will achieve important things. If they don't come, I'll keep working hard, because that's how I understand I can grow.

I'm focused and dedicated, and my result is only a consequence of my work; it's never the goal.

Without a doubt, victory is not synonymous with absolute excellence. There are one-off and occasional champions. I don't want to take away the merit of those who have dedicated themselves and won, whatever it is, but I'm not impressed by that alone. Several factors can be involved, including luck.

What defines true champions is consistency, and this is only possible when we focus on legacy. The behavior of a true winner doesn't change depending on the result.

Every time I won a World Championship, I was aware that I had only been able to hide my weaknesses from my opponents and impose a rhythm that turned the fight in my favor. I didn't win because I'm invincible or perfect, and that awareness kept me training. It happens to everyone who stays at the top of any activity: the humility to recognize that we're not perfect.

The competition that invariably pits us against our opponents brings with it another rather harmful notion. Although they are important driving forces for our development, opponents should not receive more attention than is strictly necessary, nor should they become our obsession. Studying them in order to defeat them is essential for our development, as Sun Tzu teaches in *The Art of War*: if we know the enemy and ourselves, we will not be in danger even in a hundred battles.

There is a Japanese concept called *kaizen*[21] which means being 1% better every day. Our "single objective" should be to use all the tools at our disposal to be better. The opponents will change along the way, and each of them will help us to grow in the various phases and challenges that lie ahead. And again, the focus will never be on them, but always on our own evolution.

I received my black belt with humility and respect, aware of the increased responsibility I now have as the first to be trained by master Romero Jacaré. I began to dedicate myself even more to being a good example to my young students, to climbing the rankings and standing out among the sport's elite.

***

I wasted no time. The next day, the black belt was already a reality, the long-awaited reward for my efforts and lifestyle; not an end goal. My journey had just begun, and I couldn't wait for what jiu-jitsu would have in store for me.

---

21. I recommend the books "Kaizen: the key to Japan's competitive success" and "Gemba kaizen: a commonsense approach to a continuous improvement strategy", both by Masaaki Imai.

In all my previous transitions, I'd been so prepared and above average that I'd debuted by winning championships. Now, even though I was excited to be part of a category full of idols, I knew that only the best could win.

The first competition that came up was a tournament in Petrópolis, a mountain town in Rio de Janeiro, the Blue Merlin Cup. As it was a small event, the organizers decided to combine the brown and black belts into a single category – this had only happened once before in the Cantão 4 Cup, in which I was a purple belt and couldn't fight; when Jacaré raised the flag against Royler, which led to his departure from Gracie and total dedication to our academy.

Although for me there was no advantage in taking part in a tournament with brown belts – many of whom were my old opponents – I wanted to fight and I was trained. So I signed up.

Many other black belts were left out, as it was a championship in another city and they didn't want to face the brown belts.

Although I fought in the category and the absolute, my main opponent was once again Amaury Bitetti, to whom I had already lost twice – in purple and brown.

This time, I fought like a black belt, forward, and attacked the whole fight. I had two good finishing opportunities that were well defended, and I managed to become champion. He was the greatest opponent of my sporting career and, on that occasion, our rivalry had only just begun.

I also won the absolute and my black belt debut was a success, even though I knew I hadn't faced the real champions of the time.

Training continued to be even more intense, with many hours on the mats, practicing, teaching and preparing. My days were filled with jiu-jitsu, even though I dedicated my mornings to college. I began to realize that the teaching didn't quite meet my expectations, as it was focused on generalities and school physical education.

I was looking for information on high-performance training, but I continued to attend classes believing that, in the following semesters, I would learn subjects related to my interests. I was sure that this knowledge would be fundamental for me to become a complete trainer and set me apart from other teachers – most of whom didn't study for this purpose.

With Jacaré's example and encouragement at home – my brother was finishing engineering at PUC and my sister was studying law at Candido Mendes – I insisted on going to university for a while longer.

***

The year 1990 began, and a new championship was announced in Rio de Janeiro, hosted by América Futebol Clube. Carlson's full team would be competing, and I convinced Marcelo Behring, with whom I still trained frequently, to take part as a middleweight, while I would enter as a light-heavyweight. In my category, Murilo Bustamante and, again, Amaury Bitetti, a recent black belt graduate, were entered; in Marcelo's, Bráulio Carsalade and Sergio "Bolão" Souza.

I beat Murilo in the semi-final in an unforgettable fight, in which I opened up a two-point lead at the start and managed to withstand the pressure for many minutes to win. It was my first black belt victory over one of Carlson Gracie's biggest names.

Marcelo beat Bráulio in the semi-final, but lost to Bolão in the final.

When I got on the mat with Amaury, I started losing with a takedown in the first few minutes. I was very prepared and tried everything to reverse it and, when I played guard, he tried to pass – repeating most of our fights. Amaury was very solid in this game and that's why he was such a difficult opponent. I was unsuccessful for almost nine minutes and the fight went off the mat.

The referee ordered us to restart standing, which reduced my chances – he was definitely better that way, he had already taken me down and was in his most comfortable environment. I noticed when he relaxed his grip on my kimono and walked onto the mat very confidently, as if nothing could go wrong.

I've always had reasonable judo skills and could execute a specific takedown very well (*morote seoi on* my knees)[22]. So I went in with all the energy I had left and, with a perfect projection, I scored two points and tied. With fifteen seconds to go, as there was no more time for anything, we got up for the judges' verdict. I was aware that I had been looking for more in the fight, but our perception of things is often different from that of the person judging us. A draw, I learned early on, is not a win. So if the judge decides for the other, you have no right to complain.

The referee stood between us holding our wrists as we waited for the result. Again, each judge indicated the victory of one fighter, and when I turned to the last, Carlson Gracie Jr, I realized that my chances had been drastically reduced. In a draw situation, it's unlikely that a member of the same gym will raise the flag against his partner.

The world is full of surprises, and my victory was confirmed. Master Carlson Gracie couldn't believe that his son had decided against his own school, but Juninho, as he is known, explained calmly and confidently that I had won and that he wouldn't change his vote.

I then beat two of the best fighters of my generation. On that memorable day, I confirmed that I had indeed reached black belt.

---

22. Judo projection technique.

CHAPTER 12

Master and partner

Meanwhile, my school at the Federal Club was growing. I started earning reasonable money for a young man in his twenties. I started paying for college, an important step in my independence, and I bought a motorcycle to get around the gyms more quickly, a much less intelligent decision.

At the time, I had already been presented with a car by my father. "Here's the first and last car I'm giving as a present. From now on, it's up to you," he said at the time.

When I went to pick up the bike in Alto da Gávea, the seller said he was disposing of it because he'd had an accident and fallen into the canal at the end of Leblon. He had been injured and the wounds had become infected due to the polluted water, but the vehicle was intact. There was just one problem: I didn't know how to ride, I'd never taken a driving class or anything like that. It was an adventure to get to Ipanema: I almost crashed a few times, almost fell over a few times and the engine died about five times. Fortunately, I arrived unscathed and it wasn't long before I was at ease, mastering my new toy.

***

The milestone of one hundred students, at the time, was only reached by renowned masters. I set myself this goal, which I achieved in my first year as a black belt.

My students began to excel in competitions, and I looked for ways to grow even more. The club, practically my second home, was in Alto Leblon, which was quite out of the way for the general public. I already catered for most of the members interested in training, so the most natural and logical move would be to look for a space outside the club, which I wasn't even sure was right.

Jacaré, at the time, also had around the same number of students, as the small gym couldn't hold much more than that and, to make matters worse, there were problems with the building's management. We were located in a mixed building – commercial rooms on the top floor and apartments on the other floors – where coexistence wasn't very easy, as we worked until 10pm and were probably noisy, as well as moving around the common areas of the building in a sweat.

Jacaré was already thinking of moving and this was my chance. I proposed that we combine our schools into one in Ipanema. I knew the risk of losing some of the club's pupils, but the fact was that we could look for a bigger space, which would open its doors with around two hundred pupils.

At the age of twenty-one, in my second year as a black belt, I became my master's partner. Things were happening for me, and everything only fueled my desire to work even harder.

We found the place: a building that had been closed for many years, on the first floor of the same building where Jacaré's gym used to be. The basement contained a rotating parking lot and the space was isolated, the only access to which was via a staircase. In order to access it from the first floor, where the social gate operated, whose management had been at odds with Jacaré for some time, we would have had to go to court, but the owner entered into negotiations and we reached an agreement. We got one of the biggest tatami mats in Rio de Janeiro, in the heart of Ipanema.

The venue, which had once housed a theater, was in serious disrepair and needed renovation – but we didn't have any money. There were no changing rooms, showers, etc. I sold the bike, doubled the number of private lessons and, after a few months, we opened the Master jiu-jitsu academy.

My students didn't like the news very much, as most of them lived next to the club. At the same time, they understood that it was an important development and a great opportunity for me.

CHAPTER 13

Jiu-jitsu *versus* Luta Livre

The Nastra Cup – a brand that brought products from Bali, Indonesia, and had become very fashionable in Rio de Janeiro – was supposed to be a normal championship, but it ended up changing my story and, why not say it, that of modern jiu-jitsu as a whole.

Initially, I thought I wouldn't take part, because I hadn't been training properly due to the renovations at the gym. When I went to talk to Jacaré, I heard the following phrase from the master: "Fighters fight. You can choose to fight trained or untrained. It's up to you".

I got the message and signed up. It's amazing how decisions that don't seem to matter much can change our lives.

The local press always covered the big jiu-jitsu tournaments in the city. This time was no different. The athletes were interviewed, the radio stations announced the time and place and the teams prepared for the competition.

In an interview with a Rio de Janeiro newspaper, the athlete from Carlson's academy, then a brown belt, Wallid Ismail, took the opportunity to issue a challenge to any and all martial arts, so that Jiu-Jitsu could once again prove its supremacy. Although it sounds unreasonable, this was relatively common to ensure the notion, consolidated by the Gracie family over the years by virtue of their work and victories, that it is the best form of fighting in Brazil. Most were left without an answer.

At that point, I realized that my idols were no longer showing up to fight. It was as if there was a generation *gap*, which coincided with my arrival at that graduation. I looked around and saw no one. So I thought I should take over.

The championship began and, once again, I went into the absolute final against Amaury. We were warming up for the fight when suddenly a crowd invaded the gym, a deafening noise of people shouting and pushing each other. It took me a while to understand what was going on, as I was standing on the exact opposite side of the entrance door, but I knew it was an atypical moment.

The championship was halted and, after a few long minutes, Grandmaster Robson Gracie, president of the federation at the time, took to the microphone to clarify: "The Luta Livre fighters, in a peaceful and polite way, came to our event to accept a challenge made by one of our athletes to a local newspaper. I just wanted to say to everyone present that, in keeping with the tradition of seventy years of Luta Livre and representing all those who have defended our flag so far, we have once again accepted, with the certainty that we will once again prove the superiority of jiu-jitsu".

The gymnasium erupted in shouts of "jiu-jitsu".

Meanwhile, Marcelo Behring and Master Carlson Gracie sent the Luta Livre leaders to a reserved room, letting the competition run its course to avoid any confusion that could get out of hand. I continued warming up for the absolute final, and the meeting ended with the agreement that we would have a five-match event between the Luta Livre and Jiu-Jitsu representatives.

Marcelo then went to the warm-up area and told me what had happened, including saying that he had put my name on Carlson's list so that I could compete in my first vale-tudo. I agreed without blinking an eye, but my adrenaline must have surged to levels I'd never felt before.

I went in to fight Amaury, who immediately tried to get a takedown. As he moved slowly, I was able to defend. I capitalized on his mistake to consolidate my back control, scoring four points, followed by four more when I switched to the mount, and four more when he tried to escape by turning onto his back. It was the highest score in a fight between us, who are always very evenly matched.

I won, and my mind turned to the next challenge, surely an offshoot of the clash on the beach between Rickson and Hugo that had taken place some time earlier. We had to close that chapter; it was in our hands.

***

Master Carlson was responsible for scouting and training the fighters who would represent Jiu-Jitsu. We all presented ourselves at the traditional academy on Figueiredo de Magalhães Street in Copacabana.

It was decided that we would train every day in the morning. Many other fighters showed up and, after a few weeks, the team was defined: Marcelo Behring, Murilo Bustamante, Amaury Bitetti, Wallid Ismail and myself.

On the other side, we would face Hugo Duarte, Denílson Maia, Eugênio Tadeu, Marcelo Mendes and Marco Ruas.

There were two casualties early on: Amaury contracted hepatitis and Marco Ruas quit the Luta Livre group. In the end, there would be four fights.

One of the first decisions I made was to move out of my parents' house in Ipanema so that I could concentrate fully on my training. I got a student's apart-hotel and moved to Barra da Tijuca, sharing the place with Marcelo.

I had just thrown myself into total uncertainty. While I was proud to be one of the jiu-jitsu representatives for an event of that magnitude, I didn't know what lay ahead.

I commuted from Barra da Tijuca to Copacabana every day and was never late for a workout. In the afternoons, I invested in fitness and boxing. For this, we brought champion Hélio Santana from São Paulo, one of the best boxers in Brazil – who had lost the movement in one of his arms in an accident and ended his career. He had a lot of knowledge and the mind of a champion. In Rio, he lived with Marcelo and me, helping us with our boxing technique.

It was a significant change to get on the mat and train with my traditional opponents. Although a little strange, the feeling was quickly dispelled and the group that formed under Master Carlson Gracie was basically his students, myself and Marcelo. He welcomed us very well, making us feel at home immediately.

At first, a few excited visitors came to train with us. Carlson allowed it, but he used them all as luxury *sparring* partners for the group that was going to compete. As time went by, the number of visitors decreased and only the front line of the academy continued to help us.

One of the first training sessions led by Carlson, when we still had a lot of visitors, was to put us on our guard in front of a line of about twenty fighters, who took turns every two minutes to get into our guard and try to hit us. Our goal was just not to get hit, because we couldn't fight back, nor could we reverse and get on top. Carlson told us from the first day that his concern was to make us resist on the bottom for as long as he needed to, because if we got on top, the fight would be won.

As our training progressed, I could feel my confidence rising too.

The organizers postponed the event, and a meeting was arranged at the home of Miguel Pires Gonçalves, financial director of Rede Globo, to define some points of the rules since he was involved and was an old friend of jiu-jitsu. All the fighters, their coaches, master Robson Gracie and the promoter of the fight, Carlinhos Docelar, attended.

The atmosphere was tense and, although people acted professionally, the truth was that we still hadn't got used to it. Most of us had no experience of professional fighting.

We had total confidence in Carlson and Robson to defend our interests. All the points had to be adjusted so that we could get the fight broadcast on Rede Globo.

Master Robson suggested banning closed-hand punches when the fight was on the ground, causing an immediate discussion. The Luta Livre team didn't agree with the proposal, which seemed pointless. We kept quiet, because our masters would decide.

Robson then said to Denílson, who would be my opponent: "Boy, I'm protecting you. That doesn't change anything in the fight unless you get a dominant position, like a mount. Now, I ask you: in a fight between you and Gurgel, who do you think is going to mount who? It'll be better for TV and you'll thank me".

Even so, they didn't accept and it was agreed that it would really be a vale-tudo, in two fifteen-minute *rounds*, on August 31 at the Grajaú Tennis Club.

***

Rio de Janeiro breathed this rivalry. Fights broke out between fighters on both sides and, when we heard about it, we tried to keep it professional and sporting. A few articles began to appear in the press about the future confrontation, and it seemed that the temperature in the pressure cooker was rising.

I remember once when my father asked me if I knew my opponent well. I thought it was a strange question, but he explained that an acquaintance from the club group had said that he was a very dangerous fighter, who used to throw spinal wrenches and would leave me paralyzed. I laughed immediately to reassure him, and explained that this would never happen, because I was working hard and very prepared, and that I believed it would be a smooth fight. He smiled and said that he trusted me and would be cheering me on as always.

That was just one of the many comments designed to destabilize me, to make me give up. There are cowards in the world, like those who appeal to a father's concern. In fact, it had the opposite effect and gave me even more fuel to train and prove my competence to those who doubted.

In the jiu-jitsu community, I also heard some comments about me not being the best option to represent the martial art, since I had no experience with street fights. This shows the profound lack of knowledge about the difference between a fight and a brawl.

I was officially scheduled to face Denilson Maia, and it would be my chance to prove myself.

A few weeks before the fight, Marcelo was sidelined due to an inflammation in his elbow, which was already compromising his training. There wasn't enough time for recovery, so he just carried on being involved and helping out a lot.

With three fights instead of four confirmed, Hugo Duarte – the fighter who faced Rickson on the sands of the beach – was left without an opponent.

Training slowed down so that everyone could recover from the minor injuries, and some from the infections that hit the whole gym – I myself had seven infected boils during training, as did Murilo and Wallid.

We were very well trained and even Carlson said that I had evolved and was no match for any opponent in my category. He went on to say that he didn't think I'd receive a single punch. Nobody knew the fight like he did and, once again, he proved me right.

That day will forever be remembered in the history of martial arts and I'm proud to have been part of the Jiu-Jitsu team. We did everything right and, even though I was afraid – after all, I'd never taken part in a vale-tudo fight – I was ready.

Whether we call it adrenaline, tension or any other name, the truth is that this emotion is impossible not to feel. It's up to us to decide whether to face it or run away; that's the only decision that really matters.

It's fear, a very familiar feeling to me. I lived with it every time I competed, and I was very well prepared to control it in all the competitions I took part in.

Ever since I was a kid, I always wanted my name to be written in the history of jiu-jitsu and I knew that, to do so, I would have to overcome several obstacles. This fight was the biggest yet and, although the dose of fear seemed greater, the reward would also be of another dimension.

We arrived at the gym on a bus with our team and entered through the side door without too much trouble. The surrounding area was packed with cars and people everywhere. On the way to the changing room, Master Robson had the idea – not a very good one – of going back and entering from the front, as we were the stars of the event and the crowd would love to see us coming.

It was chaos. Hundreds of people wanted to get through a door, shaking the gate to get in without paying for a ticket, while we tried to get in through a cordon. After many minutes of stalemate, we passed through to the delirious sound of a passionate crowd, the vast majority of whom were jiu-jitsu fans. We entered the changing room – which wasn't great – and warmed up on the terrace.

We talked about the importance of that moment for jiu-jitsu, the pride we should feel for having been chosen as representatives in this important mission; about the tradition and legacy built on sweat and blood for over seventy years.

We were reminded that our heroes had always put jiu-jitsu above themselves and now it was our moment to join the *hall of* greats of the art. We would defend it, and master João Alberto Barreto was certain that we would do so with honor and above our own interests. From that moment on, our bodies no longer belonged to us, and any possible accident that might cause us to break an arm, lose a tooth or open a cut would become a medal in the jiu-jitsu museum. He stressed that our corner would not throw in the towel to end the fight, wished us good luck and said: “See you in the ring!”

I entered the ring after two jiu-jitsu victories. Wallid and Murilo had already done their job impeccably and I would be the last.

I walked around the stage wearing my kimono to get a feel for the terrain. The crowd was euphoric, but I only looked at my *corner* and my opponent. Everything else was blurred.

The judge called us over for our final instructions, and I got a little closer, although I didn't want to hear any more – I knew the rules and it was time to put them into practice. We were told to go back to the *corners,* because the fight was about to start. The bell sounded and the fight began.

I was comfortable with my boxing, but I knew that this place was the only possible risk for me. After all, one hand coming in could change the whole plan. As Mike Tyson once said: “Everyone has a plan until they get punched in the mouth”.

Mine was to distract my opponent and get into the *clinch*[23]. And that's what I did. I threw a *jab* and a straight right[24]. He surprised me and, instead of exchanging punches, went into a perfect baiana[25] , taking me to the ground. I fell into guard, immediately assuming that I had left the danger zone and entered where I had trained the most.

He tried to hit me a few times, exactly as Carlson had warned and trained us, and I blocked easily. Until then, I hadn't been punched. I opened my guard and my opponent moved away.

---

23. *Clinche* occurs when fighters enter a hand-to-hand fight while still standing. It is very common in boxing to avoid the ideal distance from the opponent's punches.
24. The fighter's most powerful punch, which comes from the back hand in a straight line.
25. A falling movement in which you hold your opponent's legs to bring him to the ground.

Still on the ground, I kicked the inside of his leg, which tilted his body slightly forward. The next kick went high, towards his face, and hit him right in the neck. The crowd rose to their feet and I saw the frustration on his face, the certainty that, in my guard, he didn't stand a chance.

I seized the moment and stood up safely. With the fight back on its feet, I threw some blows and we went back to the *clinch*, keeping a safe distance. I needed to work on taking him down, which I managed to do after a few exchanges[26]. I fell on top and, in my mind, there was no way he could escape my technique.

My lungs felt huge and there was no sign of tiredness. He put me in his guard and tried to hold me down, but I started punching his ribs as hard as I could. From the *corner*, Hélio urged me not to wear myself out, but I was not fatigued, created the space and stood up.

When I hit my opponent's nose with the first good straight, still inside his guard, he opened up and tried to attack me with a footlock[27]. I defended and got back on top, now in the open guard. The fight was at a good moment and I accelerated to pass the guard. After one move, I reached half-guard and was able to move to the mount, the supreme position in a real fight. I remembered two things before I started punching from the top to finish the fight: Master Robson's speech when he tried to put a ban on punches on the ground in the rules, and my father's concern that my opponent might apply a neck lock on me. This was possibly never said by my opponent, but it was the fuel for me to throw 43 punches from the mount and finish this historic victory for Jiu-Jitsu over Luta Livre in an undeniable way.

The ring was invaded by the crowd, who lifted us up in their arms with shouts of "Jiu-Jitsu!"

---

26. Fencing exchanges happen when the two opponents seek better positioning and dominance in the *clinch*.

27. A blow that forces the ankle joint.

Moments before I got on the mat, Hugo Duarte had climbed into the ring to receive his W.O. victory against Marcelo Behring, in a totally unnecessary scene given the general knowledge of my teammate's injury. We watched this moment on the locker room monitor and I remember Carlson telling me to stay in the ring if I won the fight quickly, because he would challenge Hugo.

I never thought it would actually happen, and I took it as an incentive to show me how much he trusted me. Then, when everyone stormed the ring, he joked about it.

Anyway, I never knew if this was a plan in the master's mind or if it was really just an incentive.

Rio de Janeiro was jiu-jitsu. Our fight was broadcast by Rede Globo in prime time, we went from being known only by a niche to being recognized wherever we went. In short, our martial art exploded all over Brazil.

At the age of twenty-one, I had won the biggest event in modern jiu-jitsu history, I was my master's partner in a gym with over two hundred students in Ipanema, and I was financially independent. Nothing could make me give up these achievements. I only looked forward.

Master jiu-jitsu became my top priority. I spent all day teaching and training. College no longer had a place in my life. My breaks were dedicated to exercising on the beach. Gradually, I took control of the gym's payments and began to dedicate myself more to management, which would become both a passion and a necessity.

When I was twenty-two, I bought a car with my own money for the first time.

Even though I was one of the top black belts on the jiu-jitsu scene, I knew it wasn't enough; more than that, it was temporary. I always had to look forward and look for new opportunities.

With the success of our venture, we received an offer to got to Vitória, in Espírito Santo, to a gym called Ponto 1, which was already established in the city. Jacaré and I agreed that it would be a great opportunity, and we agreed to rotate every fortnight between us and one of our main teachers at the time, Telo.

The journey by car was on a road that wasn't very safe and, apart from a few adventures, I suffered a not very serious accident. The important thing is that we established jiu-jitsu in the city and assembled an incredible group of athletes who were fundamental to the growth of our team.

CHAPTER 14

The Alliance

I continued to fight in the championships and had a lot of success. Our academy grew. Alexandre Paiva and Traven, respectively the second and third black belts trained by the master, opened an academy together – Strike. The four of us started to face a problem that I had already experienced for a short time while teaching at the Federal Club: our students were fighting each other in the championships. The more athletes we had, the more this happened.

It didn't make sense to us, who were brought up as brothers and didn't want to be on opposite sides of the mat. We had an idea: why not bring all our schools together under one banner so that all the students who graduated from Jacaré's school could form a single team?

If we were able to organize ourselves and convince all the teachers, we'd have the best team in the world.

Some students, although not Jacaré graduates, were training with us at the time and were also involved in the project. The model would be similar to what Gracie used to do, holding selections among the fighters to decide which athletes would represent the team, since only two are accepted per belt and weight division – a rule that remains to this day.

Everyone liked the idea and we decided to compete as a single team. We started thinking about what the name would be. Normally, it's that of the most senior, but we'd talked about it before and found it a bit egoless and uncommercial. Since I became a partner in Jacaré, we decided to be neutral by choosing to call our team Master.

The thought had to be the same now: a name that everyone felt part of, that represented our unity and friendship. It should also be international, because we knew that jiu-jitsu would conquer the world sooner or later.

Among several suggestions, the name Alliance was approved without any resistance.

The time had come to sort out the logo. Back then, most jiu-jitsu academies had their own badge. Carlson had two versions: a bulldog and a rooster. Jacare, an alligator. Me, Muttley, a cartoon character dressed in a kimono. Barra Gracie, a Tasmanian devil; and so on.

When we created Master, Jacaré and I combined our logos, putting the two mascots training together.

Now we needed a logo that represented everyone and, at the same time, was unique, strong and applicable, which would be our brand. At a team meeting on various subjects, Rodrigo Didier, a school friend and student of Alexandre's, showed up with a drawing to present. From his briefcase, he took out a piece of cardboard covered with tracing paper and drew the image that is now known worldwide: a stylized eagle inside a black triangle, on which we read "Alliance Jiu Jitsu" at the base. The triangle represents solidity, balance and points upwards, the path to success. The eagle represents high flying, above everyone, an animal that has no predator.

We were all very pleased, although we still felt that we should be represented individually. We took the decision – which later proved to be wrong – to put the teacher's name on the left side of the triangle. In the end, this polluted the brand and caused us some problems.

Anyway, we had a very strong team and a new flag for everyone to represent.

In the same year that Alliance was founded as a competition team, jiu-jitsu had two major milestones: the establishment of the Brazilian Jiu-Jitsu Confederation (CBJJ) and the creation of the Ultimate Fighting Championship (UFC) by Grandmaster Hélio's eldest son, Rorion Gracie.

Until then, only the Rio de Janeiro federation held the events. With the explosion of jiu-jitsu in Brazil after vale-tudo against Luta Livre, it was more than necessary to create a national body to organize the sport. Carlos Gracie Júnior took the lead and, after some family disputes and discussions, the CBJJ was founded.

To create the UFC, Rorion Gracie used basically the same strategy he had used before to prove the effectiveness of jiu-jitsu in Brazil in the early decades of the 20th century: challenge other martial arts to a fight without rules.

In a more media-friendly way, the fights would be held in a cage – an idea inspired by the Roman Colosseum – where two fighters would enter and only one would leave. Going beyond the limits of the United States, the UFC exploded and the world got to know Brazilian jiu-jitsu through Royce Gracie's flawless performances, beating opponents of all sizes without the need to use any traumatic blows. The world woke up to the Brazilian martial art, which became an export product.

With the end of the borders and the great migration of Brazilian teachers to the USA, I understood that a window of opportunity had just opened. In addition, CBJJ started holding official championships from 1994. I was Brazilian champion.

As a sport, jiu-jitsu had reached another level. However, it began to face a problem that worsened over the years: the unbridled increase in the number of gyms with poorly prepared instructors who were totally focused on competition. The demand was so great that, not infrequently, we saw purple belts teaching classes and, of course, charging much less for it.

The market was pulled down, and the teachers – generally untrained in how to teach and run a business – didn't realize that the movement they were creating would be very damaging to everyone. All they cared about was building champions and getting their schools recognized. The whole world of jiu-jitsu was dedicated to that.

With this explosion of gyms focused on the performance of their fighters, most potential athletes began to shy away from jiu-jitsu, which slowly turned into an activity aimed at the most hardened practitioners: either you were one of them and competed, or you weren't part of the tribe and were thrown out.

There were tatami mats all over Brazil, especially in Rio de Janeiro, with very few students and no commercial success whatsoever, totally different from what I had imagined building in Jiu-Jitsu.

Alliance was a powerhouse on the sports scene, but part of a scenario that needed to change.

I've always looked to the generations before me, either to learn what to do or to avoid making the same mistakes.

Many of the big names in jiu-jitsu had migrated to the USA, and I heard stories about how they were breaking new ground. I was excited about the possibility of joining them.

However, competitive jiu-jitsu was growing in Brazil and it was important to "ride the wave". More and more, the community valued the champion of the moment, and this made me realize that if I left, I would be forgotten.

I decided to solidify my position before thinking about moving away or, better still, to keep progressing and doing relevant things without having to move away. I had this thought in my head when a friend invited me to visit some gyms in São Paulo. There was a great demand for jiu-jitsu there and the city was orphaned of a quality team.

I knew São Paulo and was aware of the city's potential, which for me had always been linked to Marcelo Behring. I hadn't even considered the possibility of a project without him, but the reality was that he was no longer teaching. I agreed to visit and I could feel the great difference in the market, the appreciation of hard work and the range of good opportunities.

On one of my visits, I went to the Fórmula gym inside the Eldorado shopping center. It was an impressive place, with three 25-meter swimming pools, a weight room with state-of-the-art equipment, a basketball court, a huge mat room and giant changing rooms. Fully equipped, it was a dream gym under the management of Ricardo D'Elia, whom I had met through Marcelo during his physical preparation for vale-tudo two years earlier. When he heard that I was thinking of maybe moving to São Paulo, he assured me that this was the place for me. He told me to stop looking and come back the next day so we could work out the financial details of hiring me. I was extremely excited. The salary, plus the payment for my private lessons, would be enough to get me started in the city.

I spoke to Jacaré, who also thought it was a good opportunity and said it wouldn't hurt to try. Anyway, if it went wrong, I could come back at any time. He assured me.

Certain that everything would work out, I packed my bags and moved out.

CHAPTER 15

São Paulo

I arrived in São Paulo with the status of a jiu-jitsu champion. I taught at Fórmula, which had a team of stars in all sports. It was a real *dream team* of professionals, very compatible with the structure of the academy.

I rented a large, expensive and well-located house, with space for mats in the garage where I could give private lessons, copying a winning model created by Rorion Gracie when he implemented jiu-jitsu in the USA.

I trained whenever I could, although I often went in early and left late at night without even seeing the sun, as the facilities were in the basement of the shopping center.

A few months after arriving, an opportunity came up to compete in a championship in Denmark. Even though the rules were different from what I was used to, it was an opportunity to take part in an international event for the first time. I was very excited. We set up the team: Jacaré as coach, Telo at light-heavyweight, as well as Sylvio Behring and some other members from São Paulo.

The fights began with karate, and we would score points if we kicked or punched the torso or got close to the face without touching. Holding on to the kimono, it became standing Judo. If it went to the ground, we could use Jiu-Jitsu to win by submission, even before regulation time.

According to the rules, we had to score points in karate, take a fall in judo and finish on the ground, all in two two-minute rounds. Even though we thought it was terrible, competing in Europe would open doors for Brazilian Jiu-Jitsu there, as we decided to organize a seminar tour after the competition.

We arrived in cold Copenhagen for the tournament in November. It was snowing, and it felt like night, due to the very little sunlight during the day. We went to the gymnasium, where several countries were represented in a relatively large event. I remember thinking how distant that reality was, perhaps unattainable for our jiu-jitsu.

Entered in the 88 kilos or more category – there was no weight ceiling above that – I faced a Frenchman weighing exactly 150 kilos. The fight began and, being much faster, I managed to land several blows to the torso. I kept scoring points while he held on to my kimono to try to give me Judo takedowns, his specialty. I attacked his legs and took the fight to the ground, where I was able to dominate him easily. By the end of the first round, I was winning easily and the fight was heading for the end.

My opponent then managed to get hold of my kimono in order to apply a sacrificial takedown called *tani otoshi* – the fighter stretches his leg out behind his opponent, sitting on the ground and projecting his weight in order to take him down. However, he missed the takedown and, instead of the ground, he sat on my knee. I managed to pull him off, but he ended up on my leg.

A dry noise echoed, like a broomstick breaking – in this case, it was my leg. With seven seconds to go, I clutched my shin with both hands, feeling the underside completely disconnect. All that was going through my head was the feeling that I had reached the end of my career.

The medical team came in, cut off my pants and put on an inflatable plastic boot which apparently held my leg in place, relieving the stabbing pain. The nurse gave my thigh an injection of morphine. They put me in the ambulance and I left the gym straight for the hospital, where I learned that I would need surgery the next morning.

In my room, unable to communicate with anyone, I thought about how to recover from it, calculating how long it would take me to fight again. In the middle of the night, the splint came off and the pain was immense.

I only woke up after the surgery, with my friends by my side. Everything went as expected, but it would still take me a few days to recover and their trip needed to continue.

Raul Gazolla, who was with us accompanying the team and documenting the trip, volunteered to stay with me. He spent a few days in hospital, often sleeping in a chair, speeding up the paperwork and coordinating the tickets so that we could return to Brazil. I'll always be grateful for that attitude, which meant a lot at the time.

Released from the hospital, I went to the airport by ambulance, and by stretcher straight to first class on a Varig flight, always with my leg stretched out. Back in Brazil, another ambulance was waiting for me.

Eager to begin my recovery and finally at home, I returned to Formula classes using crutches and taking advantage of the gym to dedicate myself to physiotherapy.

It was summer and the mats were naturally emptier. As a result, the management reduced my workload. I said I didn't see a problem as long as we resumed after the vacations. They agreed, but the impression that something wouldn't work didn't leave my head.

As I already had a few private students, this pay cut didn't hurt my budget too much at first.

The vacation was over and everything was supposed to go back to normal, but the academy's strategy was very clear – they used the big names for the launch and, after six months, dismissed everyone. In my case, I had reorganized my entire life in São Paulo – including signing an expensive rental contract.

They justified my dismissal with the private lessons I was giving at home – which were clearly discussed when I moved.

Outraged by the foul play, I wanted to tell my students in person, but I was prevented from entering the place. I felt powerless and wondered what they would say, especially worried about the possibility of my name and reputation being tarnished. Fortunately, some of my closest fighters took care to spread my version of events to the others.

I turned this page with a big problem on my hands: the rent. With no money, I had to negotiate the fine and get out of the contract. Returning to Rio de Janeiro seemed like the only option, but the taste of defeat didn't leave my mouth. I had to find a way, because São Paulo had great potential and I didn't want to give up.

During the months I taught at Fórmula, I met a lot of people. Among them, Marcelo Gurgel ended up having a special place in my life. One day, he stopped me at the gym to ask, "Gurgel from where?" I briefly explained the origin and we discovered that we really were cousins. In fact, he ended up becoming my family in São Paulo.

In that moment of uncertainty, Marcelo offered me the garage of his house to put up the mats and give lessons whenever I wanted. He said I wouldn't be in the way and that it would be a pleasure. Even though I was sure it would be a hassle – opening the garage, getting the cars out, setting up the mats every morning – I didn't see an option. I accepted the generosity and, little by little, I was included in the lunches and dinners.

I started looking for space to open a gym. I didn't have much money and the situation at Marcelo's house was temporary.

I found a huge shed in need of a good renovation. When I spoke to the owner and heard the price, I explained that I didn't have any students and that a high rent was a risk I couldn't take yet. I was already going to use my savings to renovate, so the monthly amount would be too expensive.

He proposed that I pay him 20% of the turnover and, when I retorted that I had nothing guaranteed, he said that he would take the risk with me because he trusted that I would have students.

Once the deal was done, it was time to think about finances. I sold a motorcycle I had bought months before, but it wasn't enough.

Although Marcelo Behring was my natural choice, he lived between Rio de Janeiro and São Paulo. On the other hand, Sylvio had gone to help their father, Flávio, keep the academy going, but he was dissatisfied. He was a great choice: as well as being a friend, he was also an exceptional teacher. We talked, I got the other half of the money to invest, and we agreed that we would each keep 45%. Ricardo "Franjinha" Miller, who had been helping me since I broke my leg, would keep the other 5%.

We set up the Master Jiu-Jitsu unit in São Paulo and started working with the pent-up demand. We made some movement and the students started bringing their friends.

My life got organized again, I rented a house that was much more modest than my previous one and close to the gym, I started to build a team and train with them for the competitions that came up again. I continued with the private lessons and the biggest struggle passed.

Sylvio couldn't commit and, after a while, we talked and I bought his share for the amount invested. With this matter settled, established in a huge, rather hidden shed with a stagnant number of students, I had to work even harder.

Meeting a lot of people in São Paulo, old jiu-jitsu friends and people I'd met during my Formula days, I enjoyed staying in the city more and more. Besides, I was no longer a partner in Rio de Janeiro. Life started moving again.

At that time, news of Marcelo Behring's disappearance began to circulate around the city. The last time he had been seen, in a nightclub in the Lagoa district of Rio de Janeiro, had been days before. Finally, we discovered that he had been murdered in a favela in the city, at the behest of a drug dealer, out of jealousy for his wife – who had fallen in love with the fighter.

This was the first time I had experienced death taking someone so close to me, so important, and in such a tragic way. He taught me many important things, in jiu-jitsu and in life. With him, I learned to have courage, to face challenges and not to give up. He trusted me more than I trusted myself. Marcelo was loving, captivating, and his laugh and smile are forever engraved in my heart. Marcelo left a son with dear Kirla Gracie, Kywan, whom I can call friends.

***

One day, talking to Pierre Chofard, a student from my private lessons at Marcelo Gurgel's house, I said that I thought the shed was too hidden and, since I understood the city better, I thought it should be in a better, busier neighborhood. He agreed and offered to invest.

I didn't know how to do it or how to get an investor, but the idea appealed to me. I found the property in the place we wanted – a two-story building in a well-located neighborhood. There was already a restaurant negotiating for the first floor, but the second floor was a reasonable space and building the third floor would be perfect. Pierre agreed on the spot, we did the design with an architect and, finally, it was the gym of our dreams.

We started in November 1995 with 250 students – there were sixty in the previous shed – two rooms for private lessons and a huge, ultra-ventilated mat upstairs.

Pierre would receive 50% of the profits from the business until I returned the amount invested plus 50% interest. Then it would be 20%. I don't know where I got this formula from, but he was happy and so it was agreed.

Settled back in São Paulo with a gym full of students, I continued to fight and win what I contested, winning the Brazilian double and absolute championships.

In December of that intense year, I married my girlfriend, receiving Pierre's share of the gym as a gift. I insisted otherwise, but he argued that he was happy for me. Pierre remained a partner in the contract until 2019, when I sold part of the business and we updated the partnership agreement.

Adopting the name Fabio Gurgel jiu-jitsu, I revitalized my old logo from the Federal Club days – the Muttley in kimono – and I didn't stop using the Alliance symbol, which continued to grow as a competition team.

CHAPTER 16

The first World Championship

After the wedding, I traveled to Hawaii for my honeymoon. However, it was announced that the first World Championships would be organized by the Brazilian Jiu-Jitsu Confederation in January and, according to the schedule, there would be just over ten days left after the trip for me to prepare. I even considered sitting out; after all, I'd be facing the same athletes.

I decided to fight.

The event took place at the Tijuca Tennis Club, previously reserved only for Judo. After four fights, I reached the final against Murilo Bustamante, whom I beat 5-0. That was my first world title.

At the time, we had no idea how big the World Championships would be, but the important thing is that after seven years as a black belt, I won the World Championships, the Brazilian Championships for the third time and the team championships.

A new challenge came along: Sérgio Monteiro, a friend who lived in the USA, called me to ask if I'd like to fight in the UFC. I remember being very excited and at the same time apprehensive, wondering who could train me. Our school was very focused on sport jiu-jitsu. So I called Rickson, who supported me and said he would train me.

I spoke to Sérgio, who later became my manager, and confirmed my presence at the event. The champion at the time was Coleman, who would be on the *card*[28] – the only information I had. I organized everything at the gym and, two months before the fight, I went to Los Angeles.

We got a place as an *alternate*[29] for the Traven, and set off with our boxing teacher, Claudio Coelho, staying at the house of a friend who was studying in the city. We trained with Rickson for two hours a day, apart from boxing and physical preparation. I had the opportunity to see his genius and understanding of technique up close. I learned a lot during that time.

The list of fighters was announced and names like Jerry Bohlander and Tank Abbott would be the path to the final, probably against Coleman. Rickson invited some *wrestlers* and other fighters to simulate much heavier opponents. I trained with a wrestler of about 140 kilos, really huge, but I had no difficulty. I was confident in all scenarios, showing sharp boxing and feeling infinite gas.

During the tests for the event, the doctor analyzed a problem in my electrocardiogram that prevented him from releasing me for the fight. I had a more thorough analysis of my heart and we discovered that, fortunately, it was just a tenderness. I didn't train properly for days, worried and feeling unusually tired. It's amazing how the mind can get in the way of the body.

With the doctor's release and the training regularized, the week of the fight finally arrived. Two days before I was due to leave for Georgia, Rickson informed me that he wouldn't be able to accompany me or stay in the *corner*, as there was a dispute between the Japanese organization he was fighting

28. List of fighters included in the event.

29. Reserve fighter, not included in the main card of the event.

for and the UFC. My confidence was shaken, but I understood and thanked him sincerely for his months of dedication. I promised that I would do my best to win.

Unable to believe that this was happening, I called Jacaré to ask him to stay in our *corner* – mine, Traven's and Claudinho's. With that settled, we traveled and, already at the hotel, we met several friends and students, who came to watch the event and see us fight.

After much discussion in the pre-match huddle, a fifteen-minute round was decided.

Big John McCarthy sat down with me to explain the rules, and said he knew I would be very comfortable on the ground, but if the fight was short on action, he would tell me to get up. I understood perfectly.

I fought Jerry Bohlander, a competitor of my weight from the Lion's Den school, the same as Ken Shamrock, one of the UFC's first idols. The fight started and, looking for the *clinch*, I couldn't take him down. I ended up on the bottom.

Back on my feet, I landed a straight right to his face and he bent his legs. Maybe it was time to keep punching, but I wasn't conditioned to do that. So I took the opportunity to take him down. I got into a very dominant position and went to the mount, my favorite position, willing to finish the fight.

Bohlander exploded just as I made the move, and I lost my position. He fell on top, glued to the cage, holding it with both hands and preventing me from moving away or attempting any attack. We went to the middle of the octagon and an opportunity for me to attack, but he quickly dragged me to the fence again, throwing very short punches that had no effect. At the end of the 15 minutes, never interrupted by the referee, Bohlander was declared the winner.

I felt the disappointment of losing a fight I could've won, leaving without any injuries. I didn't land any effective blows – I was frustrated. After training hard, I didn't even perform half as well.

I went back to the gym in São Paulo and found a terrible atmosphere. I heard that Franjinha, my main teacher, was extremely dissatisfied and was planning to open his own academy. I didn't believe the rumors and graduated him to black belt because I thought it was time. The rumors turned out to be true and our relationship soured when he left the academy.

I reached another delicate moment in my life: full of students and without my main teacher. On the other hand, this period opened up another opportunity with Leo Vieira, who had just won the brown belt world championship and been graduated to black belt at our Rio de Janeiro academy by Jacaré. I invited him to take on some classes and he joined the São Paulo team. We taught, trained and competed; our team gained a lot of quality.

Frederico Lapenda, a new manager, called me offering a rematch against Jerry Bohlander in Brazil. I accepted immediately and we started a big promotion. We did the *face off*[30] , recorded several promotional videos, took photos for billboards and everything else. The fight was scheduled for January 17th. Six months after the UFC, I would have my rematch.

I trained hard and was very well prepared, more experienced and with the support of my fans. Not everything goes according to plan and we have to adapt to the new situations that come our way. Bohlander didn't sign the contract and, although the promoter tried until the last minute, he didn't risk going ahead with the event, which was canceled.

Frederico then called me and offered a super fight with another athlete, and that I could suggest a name I wanted to fight. I replied that, as Bohlander wasn't coming, I'd like to test myself again in an eight-fighter tournament with three fights on the night[31].

---

30. It happens when two fighters are put face to face in front of the media to publicize a fight.
31. The championship would have eight fighters in a bracket; the champion would fight three times on the same night.

He then said that I could choose the *super fight*[32] , but I preferred to enter the tournament. So I was announced in the World Vale-Tudo Championship 3 (WVCIII).

Among the fighters were familiar UFC veterans such as Pat Smith and Paul Varelans, a 160-kilogram wrestler . When I saw who was arriving for the rules meeting, I knew that he would be my main opponent in the tournament, Mark Kerr, who was trained by Richard Hamilton, a coach who had already revealed Don Frye and Mark Coleman.

My first fight was against Pat Smith, a 100-kilogram competitor who was extremely dangerous in the standing game. I needed to shorten the distance and I mentally prepared myself to do so as soon as the starting bell sounded.

Strikers, fighters who like to fight exchanging kicks and punches, usually need time to analyze the distance before preparing their combinations. I didn't give him that time. I walked at speed and, as he tried to move in the ring to find the best distance, he was trapped. I grabbed his waist and, without taking any blows, got out of the danger zone and into my game.

I tried to take him down and I felt he was already falling when something stopped his fall: he had wrapped his arms around the ring rope – a forbidden move. The referee and I did everything we could to get him to let go, and a member of the public even pushed his arm – an obvious failure in the security of the event – but nothing happened and the position remained the same. Smith, seeing that he couldn't escape – he'd have to let go of the rope and fall afterwards – chose to give up, claiming that the fan had assaulted him.

I advanced to the semi-final.

My second fight was against Michael Patchouli, an American *wrestler* not much bigger than me. I won without much trouble in just under five minutes with punches from inside my open guard.

---

32. *Superfight* is a single fight.

In the final, as I had predicted, I faced Mark Kerr, who cleared the other side of the bracket with some very violent fights. Everyone was visibly apprehensive. As well as being big and strong, he was a top *wrestler*. The forecast was for a great fight.

We climbed into the ring and the fight began. I spent the next half hour living one of the most intense and important experiences of my career. With no rounds or rests – apart from those inside the fight due to technique – the battle was already very intense.

Kerr set out to take me down and, although I landed some good punches, fighting on the bottom was more likely to be within my plan.

When I was *clinched*, I voluntarily pulled guard so as not to be surprised by a worse takedown, and the fight went to the ground. With his weight on me, very well distributed and with a solid base, the exchanges of blows intensified.

I tried to keep a safe distance while guarding, remembering Carlson's training sessions years before and how important they had been. My confidence was unshakable, and every time I lost control of the distance because he moved away, I got up and we started again. This process was repeated a few times; and few blows got through my line of defense.

Kerr changed his strategy and began to put his weight up more, requiring me to make a lot of effort to push him away. In one of those moments, he bit my finger with all his might. I turned to complain to the referee and was head-butted below the eye.

The fight went on without any interruption, looking like a brawl. I had no one to complain to or ask for help. If I wanted to make him pay for the bite, I could hit him as cleanly as I liked, and I was already trying to do that.

Anger at his dislhonor didn't develop inside my head, nor did it become an excuse to stop. Tired, I realized that my legs began to fail as I pushed him, creating gaps in the line of defense for more blows to enter.

As my eye was swollen, my opponent pushed the swelling upwards whenever the fight slowed down. He was inside my guard, but I resisted, already almost assuming that I wouldn't be able to win.

I asked my *corner* how much time was left – twelve minutes. A few seconds of despair washed over me, because I knew I couldn't fight for that long at that intensity.

And perhaps, if I hadn't been brought up hearing stories of the sacrifices of the fighters who came before me, of the bravery and heroism with which they faced their challenges, if I hadn't been so inspired by them to be there, giving up might have been an option. I was exhausted, I could barely see, and I couldn't see any way of turning the fight around.

Choices require us to eliminate other options. When I decided to represent jiu-jitsu in vale-tudo, I chose that giving up wouldn't be a possibility. So I had to create another strategy. I couldn't keep doing the same thing.

I relaxed and stopped pushing him. I didn't resist any longer so that he wouldn't pass my guard, which happened twice and without danger. The fight changed scenery. Kerr began to slow down and get frustrated because he couldn't beat me and, little by little, I recovered. Tiredness was no longer a problem, the fight was nearing its end and I had controlled the worst moment, kept my mind strong, and kept trying to find the way to win.

The bellsounded announcing the end of the scheduled thirty-minute round and, after a short discussion about having a ten-minute extension, the judges declared Kerr's victory.

I asked for the microphone to say a few words. First, I thanked the event for the beautiful show and, above all, my students and teachers for all their support. I said that I was willing to do anything when I stepped into that ring, even go blind defending what I believe in. I remembered the words I heard in the locker room at the 1991 fight, "all the parts of our bodies would become medals in the jiu-jitsu museum", and nothing would make me prouder than to have my name engraved in that history.

At that moment, so close to my physical and mental limits, not succumbing made me a different man. I turned that defeat into one of the most important things that has happened in my career.

The following week was one of recovery and huge repercussions in the media. The fight was broadcast on Rede Bandeirantes, and articles throughout the national press highlighted vale-tudo and, consequently, jiu-jitsu.

I went back to the gym and resumed training, classes and my normal routine.

1997 had only just begun. At the age of twenty-seven, I was at the peak of my physical and technical fitness. I had always looked ahead for signs of which path to take. I chose, from a young age, to make a living from jiu-jitsu and this gave me little chance of making a mistake. We were still a small and undervalued market, I had a relatively successful academy with many students for the time and I had built up a solid reputation as an athlete and teacher.

My days were filled with what I loved doing and everything was going well. However, jiu-jitsu still had a bad image, it was attacked a lot by the media – which often highlighted fights between practitioners, making society believe that this was its main characteristic, distancing it from its origin and purpose as a tool for human development, which I had always believed in and experienced.

Fully aware of the problems, I entered a fight that was necessary for the future of the sport, although difficult to buy. Someone needed to defend jiu-jitsu from sensationalist attacks and, at the same time, make athletes and teachers aware of the need to change their attitudes.

On the other hand, the vale-tudo events were starting to get bigger and Japan had entered the circuit to compete with the UFC. Rickson had already fought a few years earlier in the *Japan Open*, but now a new event was emerging with the promise of being the biggest tournament in the sport on the planet, Pride.

I was on the crest of the wave, I had a very high-profile fight, I had the chance to pursue a professional career in vale-tudo and dedicate myself exclusively to this new sport that was emerging, MMA (Mixed Martial Arts).

Athletes from other disciplines also knew jiu-jitsu and there was no longer any need to prove that it was the best martial art against the others, what counted was the athlete, the one who could best combine the disciplines and techniques in a combat fight. It was the beginning of the individualization of sport – the fighter was more important than the art he defended.

I understood that, as tempting as it was – more money involved, the chance of worldwide fame – the being a professional fighter of vale-tudo and MMA would also be short-lived.

How many years would I still be able to fight at a high level? Five, maybe. Was stepping away from my purpose as a teacher to become just an athlete the best choice?

I decided no, that the fight I should focus on was jiu-jitsu. Although less attractive at the time, it would be much more enduring and it was what I really loved and believed in.

Gary Keller, in his best-seller *The One Thing,* says that successful results are directly related to how much you can narrow your focus. Although I believe it's necessary to dedicate yourself to what you set out to do, I disagree with this hyper-focus on just one thing. In my case, the "thing", jiu-jitsu, is a broad universe. I had to prepare myself in different skills in order to really succeed.

Just being the best fighter wouldn't get me as far. Hyper-focus needs to be temporary, and chosen very carefully. Deciding on MMA would lead me to just train and fight, compete in an extremely difficult market and, if I succeeded, live a forcibly short career.

It wasn't a good way to go.

Following jiu-jitsu, I could be an athlete without giving up teaching and taking care of the management of my academy, I could dedicate myself to organizing the Alliance and that, in itself, would bring me the need to understand business and people much better.

I saw a lot of needs ahead of me, a lot of room for improvement, and this required me to study a wide range of subjects and qualifications so that I could safely navigate all these transitions.

Throughout my journey, I've had to change positions. Adaptation is mandatory for a number of reasons. For example, as an athlete I always knew that one day my body would no longer allow me to perform satisfactorily. The natural transition would be to become a teacher, but if I waited, I would probably be a bad teacher because I wouldn't have any experience.

Ambitious people who want to evolve usually make the transition when they get good at something. A new challenge comes along and they tend to accept it, going back to being bad and having to dedicate themselves to the new role until they master it. Why not anticipate these transitions and prepare to master other skills? I've always done that.

I was an athlete, but I dedicated myself to being a good teacher. When I became a good teacher, I also wanted to be a good manager. And so on. Doing things related to the activity, even if it's not necessarily the main function, seems to me to be essential for building smooth and secure transitions.

***

The second Jiu-Jitsu World Championship was announced and, of course, I defended my title. At heavyweight, I had four fights and was champion, beating Daniel Gracie in the final.

In the absolute, I reached the final and came very close to the sport's greatest achievement, double gold at black belt. My opponent would once again be my arch-rival, Amaury Bitetti.

Our fight was as tough as ever. I pulled guard and fought from the bottom, as usual. He managed to get an advantage and came out on top. The fight accelerated and I tied it up with a near sweep.

Back on my feet, I attacked and made him leave the mat three times. I felt I was better and more whole.

We were tied at the end, and I was sure I would win on the judge's decision. With only one referee to decide, my opponent's arm was raised and Amaury Bitetti became two-time absolute world champion.

I questioned the referee, even though the decision had already been made, and I heard that the fight had been even, but as I had already won the heavyweight category, he thought it was right to give the victory to my opponent.

It was another unbelievable, unfair and revolting moment in my career.

I came out of the World Championships with a gold and a silver, even though it was my best performance at a World Championships.

Many people complain about results, and of course I have. In our desire to win, we always analyze decisions with our own bias. We often think we deserve more than we actually get, but "don't leave it in the hands of the referee", a phrase I always heard from my teacher and passed on to my students, has a very important meaning in these moments.

You must do more, make the result incontestable, completely overwhelm your opponent in order to win.

It's not always possible. There are extremely capable opponents, and injustice is not always the case. Accepting our mistakes and training to be better next time are the thoughts that drive us forward.

Complaining in order to hear confirmation from your friends of what you would like is just emotional support for a weakness on your part. Don't waste time victimizing yourself, as this can become a habit, and if it does, you'll have an almost insoluble problem on your hands.

My focus became entirely on my academy, my students and preparing them to strengthen the Alliance team in championships. Competing in jiu-jitsu and teaching at the same time had always been part of my life, and I had absolutely no problem reconciling the two.

Now, I needed to be better at management. While I was good on the mats, I was still a white belt in management, and I ran that side of the academy in a very amateurish way – just with what I had learned to do from the start in Rio de Janeiro.

I struggled to come up with new ideas and put them into practice, without an academic background in the field, even tough I'd been running my own business since I was twenty-one.

My dedication wasn't enough to avoid problems, and I came across one that I had difficulty resolving: the owner of the building where we were located wanted to double the rent – an absurdity, since I had increased the built-up area, paying for the refurbishment and legalization with the town hall.

He understood that the property had appreciated in value, and that I should pay based on the market square meter price. It wasn't fair, just as the world isn't fair, but we have to move forward with the best option we have at the moment.

Admiral McRaven, former commander of the SEALs, the US Navy's elite division, and responsible for thousands of operations during his years of service, including the one that culminated in the death of Osama bin Laden, recounts in his autobiographical book *Sea Stories* that he was once training when an order from his commander reached his ears. The word "water" meant that, whatever he was doing, he should drop and dive into the icy bay of San Diego in California. He says that he ran out, dove, rolled in the sand and returned to the formation as ordered. However, he couldn't understand why he had been given that command, since he hadn't done anything wrong.

The day went on with intense work by the entire troop, and finally everyone got into shape before dismissal. It had been a hard day as usual, made worse by the discomfort of being wet and full of sand. The commander then asked him if he knew why he had been told to jump into the water. “To show that the world isn’t fair,” said the commander.

McRaven had done nothing wrong. Sometimes the world treats us that way, and we have to decide whether to be the victim or to move on and do the best we can. The first option makes us bitter, angry at injustices and thirsty for revenge; the other makes us focus on what is in our control, teaches us that obstacles create opportunities, makes us grateful.

The good and the bad are not absolute. What seems very bad today will often do us unimaginable good in the future and, because this happened, it will allow us to achieve things we never dreamed of.

So, unable to pay the price charged by the landlord, I left the property. I remember the sense of failure I felt at not being able to keep running a gym that had been built with an ideal model in mind. For me, the only explanation was my managerial incompetence.

With two hundred students and a great reputation, I needed to move on and find a new place to teach. Being back inside a large fitness academy seemed better, as I would have to deal with much less bureaucracy and could devote myself solely to the classes and the students.

I saw an opportunity to move, with a good deal, into the Acqua Project, a very well-located gym in a place that has become the financial center of the city.

Everything improved. I no longer had to look after the facility, staff, cleaning, bills, etc. I had a space for group classes, another for private lessons and an office. I kept my company running and rented out the space, paying 20% of the turnover as rent.

The team grew and Leozinho had the idea of bringing in Tererê to help him with the classes. There were the three of us, Leo Negão, Telles, Demian, Beto Schumaker along with many others. I set up a space for private lessons, in order to provide more comfort and privacy for my students, and rented a house next door where I moved my office.

I taught classes all day, leaving Leo and Tererê in charge of the groups. I started having financial difficulties again; costs were rising steadily and turnover was gowing.

I only noticed the drop after a few months: the two hundred students had dwindled to less than a hundred. What's more, the cost of the office increased, as the boys, Leo, Negão and Tererê – who lived across the street in a rented house – used it to do privates after hours. They didn't do it out of malice or dishonesty, but the lack of administrative control on my part allowed a lot of things to go wrong, including successive teacher delays and absences.

Another failure was looming and I had to make changes. I went back to teaching group classes and dismissed Leo and Tererê – but not before passing on a group of private students and getting a place for them to start their own gym.

These measures were necessary, although they weren't well received. I left the apartment I was living in, from where I had to travel in traffic to get to work, and moved to a place closer to the gym.

I got my finances back on track and had some peace of mind.

CHAPTER 17

Jiu-jitsu around the world

One day, a visitor from Finland arrived at the gym, a Nokia director working in Brazil, a black belt in Ju-Jutsu, a sport I had competed in Europe years before. He knew almost nothing about Jiu-Jitsu, but he was delighted with our technique and asked if I would like to come to Helsinki for a seminar.

With the official invitation, I went to Finland for the first time for a seminar, on a Saturday and Sunday in May, late spring, with the sun shining practically all day until almost eleven o'clock at night. The event was packed – there were over a hundred people on a giant tatami mat, the like of which didn't exist in Brazil.

Once introduced, I began. My English was very poor, but I was able to show the techniques for four hours non-stop over the two days. I passed on a lot of information that was impossible to assimilate, but it was a success. I was invited back at the end of the year, and I made a plan.

The next time I was invited, I offered to stay for a week instead of two days, and explained that it would be much more productive if I could replicate the same rhythm of classes as my academy in São Paulo. That way, the students could learn within our model. He argued that he couldn't afford to pay more, and I replied that I wasn't thinking of earning more, just of delivering a more productive system.

The plan worked and was actually much better. Finally, we created a Brazilian Jiu-Jitsu division within the European academy. It was the Alliance's first branch outside Brazil.

We also grew in our country and, while we were trying to organize the rules for using the brand, we held endless meetings to decide what direction to take. There were too many heads without a defined leadership, and ideas never got off the ground – not even the good ones. There was no *benchmark* for a fighting organization, and the only inspiration I had was to study a little of Mestre Camisa's Abada Capoeira model, which is spread all over the world. In it, students paid a fee to join, and this fund supported the teachers who traveled and promoted the group.

With this idea in mind, I wrote a charter about how I thought the Alliance should work, presented it to Jacaré on an occasion when he was passing through Rio de Janeiro, and made a point of talking it over with several colleagues before putting it on the table. I arrived at the meeting and started telling him about the plans, as well as how I thought we should work. I proposed a monthly fee to be paid by all academies linked to the Alliance, a minimum fee for all students to have a card, the continuation of Alliance News – an internal newspaper that we would distribute to all schools – a president who would centralize all decisions and who would be elected by a vote of the founders, among other things.

When I finished making my presentation, those who had previuosly supported me were against it, saying that it was too many changes and that it wouldn't work. Finally, Jacaré decided to put a purple belt as competition manager to organize the team at the championships. My plan was totally rejected.

While I envisioned a large network with an organized team, nobody wanted to change anything at all. I put the "guitar in the case" and went back to work in my space in São Paulo.

In the first championship with the new manager in charge, everything went wrong, even the registrations. There was no support. We went back to the old pattern of decentralized organization and each academy looking after its own students.

1998 continued to be a difficult year for me, and I lost the final of the heavyweight category at the World Championships to Saulo Ribeiro. On the other hand, with Alliance, we were team world champions for the first time.

The first time I went to the USA, in 1989, I forged a close relationship with Rickson – I organized a seminar for him in São Paulo in 1995 and we started training together whenever possible. I learned a lot and will be forever grateful to him.

During a training session in Teresópolis, a mountain town in Rio de Janeiro, for one of his fights – which never took place – he came to talk to me about how his brother Royler was worried about our relationship, because he could one day face me, and he didn't like the idea of Rickson continuing to teach me.

I explained that Royler was much lighter than me – him, featherweight; me, heavyweight – but he insisted that it could happen in the absolute. I promised not to fight him, and to give up the win if we crossed paths in any championship. Rickson agreed, and promised that no student from the school would fight me. Not for that reason, but I accepted, since my aim was solely to continue learning from him.

A friend called me asking me to organize a Royce seminar in São Paulo, because Grandmaster Hélio Gracie was also going, along with Grandmaster Rorion Gracie. I promptly said yes, and did so with great success.

At the time, there was an internal rivalry between the family: Rickson and Royler on one side, Rorion, Royce and Grand Master Helio on the other. I, of course, had no idea and this was never told or explained to me. Today, I see that Rickson understood that I couldn't have organized Royce's seminar.

Saulo, who was Royler's pupil, signed up for my category without anyone saying anything. He got to the World Championship final with me. As I hadn't asked for anything, I didn't expect anything. That was the end of the deal and Rickson and I grew apart. I have enormous admiration, respect and gratitude for him, but our paths parted.

I lost the individual championship, but the Alliance team won its first title in thrilling fashion. We were playing point for point with Barra Gracie, and the categories had already been closed.

In the last one, the absolute purple belt, we didn't have anyone heavy – which reduced our chances. However, we had a kid who would make a lot of noise in the jiu-jitsu world: our lightweight, Fernando Tererê. He started off well, winning his first fight, but came up against Alexandre Café, from Barra Gracie, a very good super-heavyweight athlete. The fight went as expected, with a big advantage in Café's favor. There were no more real chances of a comeback, the "shovel of whitewash" was about to be placed. Café went for an armbar and finished Tererê, who tapped immediately. His arm continued to be squeezed even after the referee's intervention, in an extremely unsportsmanlike attitude, which led to Café's disqualification and Tererê's unexpected victory.

We were through to the semi-finals, but the problem had grown in size. The opponent was now the feared Ricco Rodriguez, 120 kilos, *wrestler* and exceptional competitor – who later became the star of the Abu Dhabi Combat Championship (ADCC) and UFC.

It was another horrible fight for Tererê, who was trailing 13-0 until the last few seconds, when they managed to break out of an attack and, for the first time, come out on top.

Ricco was forced to turn around on all fours to protect himself from a guard pass, and took a devastating blow to the neck. There was no time left and no one believed he would tap, but the referee noticed drool in Ricco's mouth and noticed that the athlete was unconscious, ending the fight. Tererê was declared the winner and went on to an almost impossible final.

We now had another direct match against Barra Gracie, Rolls Jr., a fighter who also had the weight and size advantage. Everything seemed to be working out for us and, with hope, we watched Tererê get on the mat. He started by losing once again.

Towards the end, he was playing guard unsuccessfully with his sweep attempts, all of which were well defended by Rolls' son. Tererê then found a triangle choke[33] and, being much lighter, couldn't prevent his opponent from standing up to defend.

It was his last chance, and our representative went up with the triangle half-covered, hugging his opponent's neck, who didn't think twice and threw himself to the ground with all his might, executing the pile driver, a forbidden move I've mentioned before, and being immediately disqualified.

Tererê was the absolute purple belt world champion and Alliance was the team world champion for the first time by a difference of just two points.

As world champions, the Alliance attracted even more attention. I tried to capitalize by increasing our network of affiliates in Brazil and, above all, in other countries. New York and Helsinki were the first cities, followed by Frankfurt and Berlin. Soon we had a network that occupied me for several weeks of the year. I traveled, got to know the world and came back with a good amount of money in hard currency, which I used to build up savings.

Each of the Alliance founders did or tried to do the same thing, some more successfully, others less so, but our team grew in size in a disorganized way, even as we became more and more present and relevant to jiu-jitsu.

---

33. Very fast and unexpected movement to land the blow.

In 1999, we had a great championship and won the World Team Championship again. I didn't win the title again. At the age of twenty-nine, I fell in the semi-finals in a fight against Murilo Bustamante, that year's champion.

I managed to organize a training center in the interior of São Paulo, and took our almost complete team – around sixty athletes – to train for ten days, eating and sleeping 100% focused on the main jiu-jitsu tournament. I did all the training, but I didn't manage a good performance.

My personal life was in disarray – I'd just split with my wife and was enjoying the feeling of freedom, devoting far less time to my practice than I should have. Ten, twenty or thirty days of dedication doesn't erase everything that was done wrong.

I often say, as I learned from Bené when I was playing volleyball, that you can never make up for a day's lost training. This doesn't mean that you can't make an effort, but you'll never make up for what you've missed. That's why, when we talk about discipline, we need to understand what it really means and how we can put it into our lives once and for all. Undoubtedly, it won't prevent defeats, but it will bring the certainty of having done your duty, which is almost the same thing.

"Discipline is freedom". Perhaps you've heard this phrase before, and it's very true in the sense that we first need to control our impulses and passions. This is the first and most important task in becoming a disciplined person.

Temptations are everywhere and must always be resisted. In the example of dieting, eating a sweet now and then is not bad for your health, but it does undermine your confidence in controlling your desires. Every time we give in, we weaken ourselves, we deviate from the path of discipline and, consequently, from virtue.

People often label as radical those who always choose what is best, belittling their efforts. Achieving control, like everything else in life, is a matter of training, and can be started at any time and adopted in different aspects of life.

Improving our diet is just as important as exercising, which doesn't come ahead of intellectual development. And none of this will lead us to a virtuous life if we don't know how to relate to others, take care of the people around us, make ourselves available to our family and friends and so on.

Discipline allows us not to spend time on things that don't matter. Seneca said, in *On the Shortness of Life,* that "it is not life that is short, it is we who spend our time in the wrong way".

Dedicating yourself to being the best you can be every day is a way of life, and keeps you away from the dangers that are increasingly constant in our society. Immediate pleasures and the law of minimum effort are evils created by the development of new technologies, which lead us to a life averse to any sacrifice and an eternal search for happiness based on hedonistic concepts. There is no satisfaction in achievement preceded by determination and effort, but pleasure for pleasure's sake, which makes us weak and empty of feeling.

I was totally focused on jiu-jitsu, following my students fighting in Japan, some of them making it big in the UFC, and dedicated to growing my school. I got an extensive portfolio of private lessons and conducted an average of ten workouts a day, as well as practicing for two more periods – including physical preparation, divided between weight training, running, stairs and sprints on the track. I took the students with me, without speacial treatment for anyone, and that's why I got the nickname General from Leo Negão.

I was invited to fight in the second edition of the ADCC, in the up to 88 kilos category. It was Jiu-Jitsu once again taking me to see the world, now in the United Arab Emirates and fighting another type of sport, certainly more similar than the one in Denmark in 1993. Several jiu-jitsu names were present. In my category, Amaury, Renzo and Libório represented Brazil. Unfortunately, we lost to two Russian *wrestlers* who made the final.

After that, Abu Dhabi became a huge jiu-jitsu hub, and that's where I had many experiences.

At the age of thirty, I still felt in top shape and my mind kept thinking of possibilities for the jiu-jitsu market, which is still in a very difficult phase in terms of its image.

The art was discredited as a possible good business and I, who disagreed with this understanding, didn't see a clear path or anyone thinking more broadly about growth. There were isolated cases and successful individual projects, which were usually "chicken flights", with no significant impact on the fighting community. The market, although better, was still very small and fragile, and that worried me.

The 2000 World Championships brought in a new generation, as the previous year's brown belt champions moved up to black belt. Many were very talented. Jiu-Jitsu was changing and evolving technically very quickly.

I started the championship with a truncated fight, which I won in the last few seconds with a sweep. Even so, it was a bad start.

I won the second without any problems and qualified for the semi-finals. At that point, after a tough win against Roberto Godoi, an opponent from São Paulo, my body cooled down and I realized that I had a very strong muscle contraction in my trapezius.

The final, broadcast by Sportv, wouldn't take place for another four hours, but the contracture got worse and worse and I opted to keep warming up with massage and ointment.

I went in to fight my fifth world final against Ricardo Arona, a super-talented athlete from Master Carlson's academy.

I managed to get a takedown that gave me the advantage. He changed his strategy, pulling me into his guard and trying to apply a triangle. However, my positioning didn't allow me to escape. I waited patiently for him to tire. When he had to let go, I was already very advanced in the position and I consolidated the guard pass to score three points and take the title for the third time.

Unfortunately, Alliance didn't manage to repeat the feat as a team. As in previous years, when I won, the group didn't win the title and vice versa. In a way, I've been champion every year.

The World Championship has established itself as jiu-jitsu's biggest party and the sport's most recognized title.

This victory opened other doors for me, and I continued to be invited to more and more seminars. In Finland, in addition to the unit in the capital, we opened others in Turku, Oulu, Porvoo, Pori, Hämeenlinna, and we now have seven affiliates in the country, which has become our main hub outside Brazil.

Whenever possible, I would visit Germany and some other new country to try to increase our network.

During those seminar weeks, I was extremely isolated, without friends and meeting the students only at training time – very early in the morning and in the evening, with very few exceptions. For them, the best season was winter, but the company of the cold didn't help me much. It was an important phase for the internationalization of the Alliance and jiu-jitsu as a whole.

CHAPTER 18

An *insight*

In a conversation with a second degree white belt student, he told me how fascinated he was with Brazilian Jiu-Jitsu, that he already came from a martial arts background and was a master of Wing Chun, a kind of Kung Fu that until then I had been completely unaware of. He said that although he loved the classes, he found the activity very intense and difficult for him, he was already in his fifties. Our training consisted of a strong warm-up, with lots of gymnastics and specific movements, some techniques and at least 45 minutes of sparring. It was really exhausting, but I had never stopped to think about it, and I even thought it was what made jiu-jitsu so effective.

The conversation continued and he wanted to know how many students we had at Alliance, information I didn't have. We were just a competition team. I felt a little embarrassed, but said that I thought we had about fifteen hundred students. He laughed and asked if I had any idea how many students his Wing Chun master had in Germany alone: fifty thousand.

How could a style that nobody knew about, that has no recognized efficiency, have such a huge number of students and jiu-jitsu so few?

I asked him to take me to a class at one of the chain's gyms. He offered immediately and we arranged a visit for the following day.

As soon as we arrived at the gym, I realized that the atmosphere was quite different from what I was used to. Everything was organized and quiet – typical traits of Japanese culture. The class began and he explained to me that the class levels were separated. The initial program was taught in one room while the more advanced ones trained in another. It was a very light activity in physical terms and, as far as I could tell, without any real combat effectiveness. So what was the trigger for so many students to seek out the sport?

The practitioners took a different color card from each other and handed it in at reception. My friend then explained how the program was divided, from white belt to black belt, and they were fully aware of what they needed to do to reach the next level and continue on the path to their graduation.

In jiu-jitsu, students never knew where they were on the journey. In order to graduate, they depended exclusively on the teacher who, more often than not, had no way of knowing exactly how far they had progressed. So they treated everyone equally.

At the time, the division of levels wasn't prioritized either; after all, it was much easier to teach a single class to everyone and whoever survived would make up the competition team – the metric that was really valued.

I thanked him for his visit and we left. My head was boiling with ideas in front of an ocean of room to grow. Jiu-Jitsu was doing everything wrong.

The evolution of the sport I loved had corrupted the art's philosophy of teaching the weakest. We were a hostile environment for 99% of the population, which explained why jiu-jitsu was not a good business: we had developed a martial art for very few, and we ourselves were responsible for that.

I disagreed with Grandmaster Hélio Gracie, who criticized the championships and said that it wasn't his jiu-jitsu, but the truth is that he was right.

We couldn't go back in time. I needed a path that would recover tradition without losing evolution. The sport was already fantastic, developing new techniques and delighting thousands of people around the world, but times had changed and the simple need for self-defense didn't seem very attractive to a civilized people – like the Finns, for example.

The first idea was very clear: the beginner would need to be separated in order to have a calm first contact, away from the risk of injury. With this in mind, we would draw up the student's lesson plan. The Gracie Academy's self-defense program seemed appropriate, but how could we put it into practice in a heterogeneous class, with different levels and experiences?

With five lessons, a student has already mastered a good number of techniques, a far cry from a beginner with fewer lessons. I needed to solve this equation, and I embraced the challenge.

I decided to start with the trivial: a program of techniques to cover the "initial" phase. I didn't need to create anything, as I remembered my beginnings and knew self-defense backwards and forwards. I organized the techniques in such a way that it would be possible for the students to train together, and no longer individually with the teacher's help. I removed a few at first.

Within a few weeks, I presented an outline of 25 classes, the backbone of our methodology, and I was very excited about the possibility of this changing Alliance – and why not? – jiu-jitsu as a whole.

CHAPTER 19

The "crack"

Back in Brazil and ready to start putting the new ideas into practice, another piece of news came to take my mind off things: rumors that the owners of the Acqua Project were going to sell the property to a construction company, and that everyone would have to leave soon. Like me, many great professionals were tenants of the space.

Meeting with Fabio Guimarães, a firness trainer from Rio with many students, and Kiko Frisoni, a squash teacher, we decided to get ahead of the game before the threat materialized. We went in search of a building to set up a gym together, and found an old car dealership, a huge place that could accommodate all the disciplines with ease.

We offered it to a fourth partner, who would be the investor, and he loved the idea. Before we even got the project off the ground, the sale of the Acqua Project building was announced. We were racing against time.

In the midst of these doubts and uncertainties, and with the World Championship approaching, I continued to train very well. At the time, my mind was already very divided between being an athlete and pursuing my plans to grow the academy and the business. In the championship, I won the qualifying rounds and reached the final with an Alliance student.

It was common – and would remain so for many years – for the oldest athlete to take the title. So we made a fight for live television, with a certain outcome. I won my fourth world jiu-jitsu title.

I decided to announce my retirement from official competitions because I was focused on building my school and being the best teacher I could be.

The methodology, which was my main project, would still have to wait a while, as the Olímpia gym, which was exactly one block away from the Acqua Project, had ended the contract with the jiu-jitsu team that worked there. The room was empty and the owner contacted me.

The negotiation was quick and simple, and we struck a deal that was very similar to the one I already had. Without this weight on my back, I was able to put my plan into practice.

We moved into the room on the first floor of the gym in February 2002. It was seven meters wide by about 25 meters long, with space for a great mat at the front and the office at the back. A curtain separated the private classroom.

Changing location is always delicate for a gym, but it seemed that we would be entering a period of tranquillity. The Acqua Project students came without difficulty. So I set up the first course with the black belts to talk about the project.

My plan seemed simple to execute and, with the methodology in hand, I just needed to teach the athletes and teachers how to work the methodology. After that, we would definitively separate the classes into beginners and advanced, and solve one of the biggest problems in jiu-jitsu at the time.

I organized the first methodology class and had a great turnout, with dozens of black belts on the mats wanting to learn how to teach. But it wasn't going to be that easy, because the vast majority didn't know basic techniques, not even self-defense. So they would have a hard time.

I recognize that this is a consequence of my failure as a teacher – although I had a great competition team, I hadn't taught jiu-jitsu in its entirety, or even the fundamentals.

I decided to implement the beginners' program in all the classes, even the advanced ones, and the competitors would do the basic techniques for a while. I personally taught each one, and the class quickly got used to a new way of understanding the martial art.

Everything seemed to be in place, the gym began to grow in number of students – especially beginners, who now had their own class and a much more comfortable start to their journey.

It was time to start thinking about how to replicate the method. The path is tortuous, and I was plunging into another difficult moment in my career.

It all started with an unusual phone call from the sponsor, the leader of Nova União. Luisinho was a well-known figure in jiu-jitsu circles, and we had a good relationship. He took care of the team's bureaucratic and political issues, but he never had any representation in the sport. I myself never saw him in a kimono, and the leaders of NU, for me, were always my friends Dedé Pederneiras and Wendell Alexander.

In practice, Luisinho spoke on behalf of the team and, right at the start of the conversation, he pointed out that Carlos Gracie Júnior wanted to be the owner of jiu-jitsu, that he didn't share anything with the athletes, and that it was high time we paid cash prizes to the winners. His idea was to organize a championship to show how it could be done.

The whole argument with Carlinhos started when Luisinho missed the deadline to make changes to his team in a recent championship, which hurt his team. It was common for teams not to submit their rosters until the last minute so that they wouldn't be surprised by a targeted line-up, but he missed the deadline and the federation wouldn't allow him to make changes.

Our phone call continued in a very cordial manner. He explained his ideas and I asked how he would put them into practice. I suggested scheduling it for a different date from the official championship, because there was no point in splitting up a sport that was still so small. It would harm us all. On another date, people would have a chance to compare the events, and the best would stand out. The competition would also be good for the athletes, who would have another competition option, and for the federations, which would need to develop. He disagreed, because he wanted to confront and destroy the institution run by Carlinhos.

I explained that I couldn't support a movement that would divide the sport because of personal motivation, that I had absolutely nothing against him, but that the Alliance wouldn't go along with it, although he could count on us if he decided to hold a championship away from the official calendar.

Before hanging up, he said that he had spoken to several of our athletes, that they would have loved it and committed to fighting in his championship. I ended the call gently, pointing out that he shouldn't have done that. I would speak with my competitors.

The fighters arrived at the gym for their midday training session, which went ahead as normal. Afterwards, we sat down to talk while still on the mats.

I told them about Luisinho's call and, in fact, they were already aware of the plans for a parallel championship to the Brazilian Team Championship – which would be held for the first time in São Paulo -, a traditional and important tournament in the calendar. Luisinho had decided to hold his championship on the same weekend, in Rio de Janeiro.

The athletes were excited about the possibility of receiving a cash prize, but I explained the harm of having another federation in the sport, that this movement was motivated by a personal dispute and probably wouldn't get very far.

I pointed out that it wasn't a fight we should buy, but they – in their dream of fighting "professionally" – had a hard time seeing that it wasn't the way to go, that dividing the sport would take us away from a possible true professionalization, and that the situation, like so many others, was just about someone with money wanting to become relevant in jiu-jitsu.

I stressed that if the event was on another date, we'd have no problem taking part, but going against the Brazilian Confederation didn't make sense.

Many athletes from São Paulo remained unyielding, as did some from Vitória and Rio de Janeiro. The issue escalated and suddenly we had an impasse.

Since everything in the Alliance was decided by a vote, we called the founders together. By counting the votes of the five present, my position won out and we decided not to take part in the championship. But the confusion had only just begun. The athletes didn't accept this and went to Luisinho to ask him to change the date of the championship or they wouldn't be able to take part.

As the main objective was to confront the CBJJ championship, Luisinho didn't agree. The most he gave in on was the schedule: instead of the black belts fighting on Sunday, they were moved to Saturday. With this concession, the athletes called Jacaré and Vinicius Campelo (who didn't attend the meeting) with the argument that the date had changed and that now there would be no obstacles. The two agreed and the discussion resumed.

The athletes insisted that their position was that of the majority. Even with the explanation that their votes would be worthless if all the arguments weren't put on the table, and even in the face of the possibility of problems with the Alliance, they took part in the two championships. They lost.

We'll never know if they would have won if they had followed the initial decision, but the real problem was that they overstepped my authority as a teacher.

The week began with the need to set the record straight. I was feeling betrayed, so I called the people involved – Fernando Tererê, Demian Maia and Eduardo Telles. I sat down with the three of them in my office and asked them what they thought of the whole situation. Each raised a different argument.

Money, freedom of choice, a feud with Carlinhos and the certainty that CBJJ was a monopoly, the fact is that there was no consensus. They weren't together for the same cause, which I only understood years later when I finally got over the episode.

At that moment, I had to show them that things didn't work like that. I resisted the urge to expel them from the academy forever – they were dear students and I loved them – so I proposed that they be suspended for ninety days. They accepted immediately, perhaps because they were expecting a much greater punishment.

But the suspension period would coincide with the World Championship and I found myself at another impasse: in my mind, they were out. Not in theirs. The problem was far from over.

During those three months, the climate became bad and a movement began to emerge among the athletes against my position, including some stories about them and Leo Vieira getting back together, who hadn't been in the gym for a long time. The rumors grew and I could feel the pressure cooker about to explode. My leadership was being called into question, my team was turning against me and I had no idea how to reverse it.

The date of the World Championships arrived, and the new confederation, CBJJO, scheduled its own championships for the same day. The three students were suspended and couldn't fight in either.

I told them that if they opposed the ban once again, I would have no choice but to remove them from the team. Even though my speech was only directed at the three of them, almost all the players showed solidarity and took another stand against me.

There, I found myself trapped: either I allowed them to participate and lose my authority, or the team split up. As painful as it was, the first option was unthinkable. The team broke up.

The World Championships totally lost it's importance given the scenario that was shaping up for our team. Finally, Luisinho seemed to have achieved his goal: he had divided the sport and created a competitor for the IBJJF World Championships, which were now empty.

The Alliance didn't stand on the podium for the first time in history, and neither did I, retired from competition.

I often felt alone and totally helpless, but I was aware that I was on the side of the truth. The narrative constructed by the athletes was based on a lie – that I had told them that, if there was no scheduling conflict, they could take part in both.

But my point was clear from the start: I wouldn't support a measure that divided the sport for a strictly personal reason, after all, a change of time wasn't a change of date, and you don't fight one championship in the morning and another in the afternoon.

I was approached by many "leaders" who, despite openly supporting them, confessed that they only insisted on the issue because they wouldn't abandon their comrades.

For a moment, I even considered leaving the Alliance. That would be the end of our team and I'd have to start again on my own – or with whoever wanted to be by my side.

But the bond I have with my master wouldn't be broken like that. I wouldn't spit the same venom at those I criticized, even in a time of difficulty, regardless of whether or not he took a stand in my favor. No matter how bad I felt, walking away from Jacaré was never a possibility.

However, Jacaré was also a direct teacher of several who were now on the opposite side of the spectrum to me. And he, outside Brazil and far away from events, preferred to wait. He stayed where he was and didn't take sides.

Even though it wasn't what I had hoped for or wanted, I saw a possibility of success, a light at the end of the tunnel. Time would play in my favor.

I carried on doing my job and looking after my gym, letting things take their course. Fights broke out between the dissidents, including over Jacaré's lack of a clear position.

One day, one of the members of the dissident group sent an impudent email to the master, accusing him of being "on the fence", saying that he had to decide between the whole group or me. They tried, in the height of the arrogance that inhabits the minds of the ignorant, to pressure him into doing their bidding. It had the opposite effect and Jacaré, who certainly had a clearer view of everything that was going on, announced that Alliance was the only team he was attached to.

At that point, I already knew it was only a matter of time, but I can't deny that I was happy and relieved to be able to count on Jacaré for the future.

2003 went on in a heavy and sad way. It was hard to believe that our team had split up so drastically and unexpectedly. A mixture of anger, disappointment and fear that my life project was doomed to failure came bitterly down my throat.

The competition team has practically all left, leaving only the athletes from my academy. Of these, some received calls and invitations to leave our academy. Few accepted.

CHAPTER 20

Marcelinho shines

The gym was in a bad mood, with no energy and few students. Our team was down to Marcelo Garcia, who was not yet a black belt – although he was recognized as a talent, since he had won championships in previous ranks.

The group that left Alliance tried everything to take him, but he resisted, saying that he had moved to São Paulo to train with me and didn't intend to change his plans. The athlete decided to stay, and this gesture was of great importance to our history. Marcelo went far beyond being one of the most dedicated and disciplined students I've ever had: he rescued me from the sadness of the ingratitude I felt.

I understood that there was someone I could help, someone who didn't deserve any bitterness from me. I quickly returned to training and we went on to win victories together. Marcelinho was everyone's role model at the academy and our team timidly began to grow.

We received an invitation to fight at an event in Campos dos Goytacazes, in the interior of Rio de Janeiro, but he wasn't very excited. I encouraged him because I knew there would be big names there and, although the logistics were terrible, he went.

It was a tournament without a kimono, a discipline in which he still didn't have much experience, as he had started training with us in São Paulo as a brown belt. Not long before, Tati, my student and his girlfriend at the time (now his wife, mother of his children and a black belt), brought him to a no-gi class at the Acqua Project.

He became the great champion and the protagonist of a very tough tournament full of stars. The title opened up the opportunity to take part in the ADCC selective in Rio.

Once again Marcelinho was the sensation of the championship, finishing all his fights until he faced a tough and frustrating fight. We lost the only spot to Daniel Moraes. As always, win or lose, our lives went on as normal the following week.

A few months later, the official ADCC event was held in São Paulo. With no athlete in contention, I booked a lecture for a company in Bahia.

On Thursday night, the organizer of the selection, Marcello Tetel, called me to find out if Marcelinho would be at the weigh-in the next day, because an American hadn't been able to get on board and he had a spot. Without blinking, I contacted Marcelinho: "Get your sneakers and go to the gym, you're going to fight in the ADCC!".

He didn't even question it, but he came in almost 3 kilos overweight. He practiced running and dehydration to beat the official 77 kilos and the next morning we were inside the ADCC.

From Bahia, I followed Marcelinho's two victories that day on the phone – Shaolin and Renzo Gracie. I've never wanted to be in one place so much, so I flew back to São Paulo early on Sunday morning to watch the finals.

He won the title in his category and, as what has always set him apart from the rest is his insistence, he also signed up for the absolute and reached the semi-finals, only to be stopped by Pé de Pano.

The world saw that shy, extremely talented boy. There began one of the most successful careers in jiu-jitsu and a new era in the understanding of how to fight without a kimono. Marcelinho revolutionized the butterfly guard[34] and the X guard[35] , created the *one leg* X guard[36] , the *seatbelt* on the back[37] among many other techniques.

We had indescribable moments of joy and success together. I've experienced a connection I've never had with any student, and every victory has been a source of great pride and celebration. We've also had painful defeats, but we've built a relationship.

I am extremely grateful for the trust Marcelo Garcia placed in my work, and for his generosity in understanding how much I needed that support.

His friendliness and competence took him far and, wherever he is, my heart goes out to him. Alliance is definitely only what it is today because it had Marcelo Garcia at the time.

The story that became known as the "Alliance rift" taught me important lessons, even if they weren't immediately assimilated. It was all very painful at first, but time has helped me to turn the bad feelings I had at the time into positive things. Today, I'm grateful for what I learned.

We've already talked about the tendency we have to categorize things as good or bad as they happen in our lives, almost always based on the moment and the impact they have. For example, I wanted to have the best team and the best jiu-jitsu school. When I lost some of my main students and athletes, I saw it as a very negative event.

Over time, I realized that everything that happened made it possible for me to organize my school using the method I had created in a smoother way, with less resistance. Because

---

34. Technique in which the fighter who is on his back on the ground uses one or both feet inside the legs of the opponent in front of him.
35. This is a variation of the hook guard, in which the legs are crossed in an X shape.
36. Variation of the X guard.
37. It's a hold using your arms around your opponent's torso with the aim of sticking to their back.

those players left, I had the opportunity to build and strengthen relationships, as in the case of Marcelinho.

Whenever something happens, we have the chance to discover a new path that we hadn't thought of before. The philosopher and Roman emperor Marcus Aurelius, in *Meditations,* said: "The obstacle is the path, what impedes action advances action, what stands in the way becomes the way".

In order for this to become a reality and for us to get the best out of every situation, regardless of whether it seems good or bad, we have to look inwards, accept our guilt for having put ourselves in that position. At the end of the day, we are the ones who let people down.

That event changed me and made me a much better person, I saw the reasons why everything had happened the way it did, and I recognized that I was partly to blame for that outcome.

Jiu-Jitsu was very small back then, and the possibilities weren't many. Those who were lower down the hierarchy used to feel that the opportunities would never come, and this may have motivated them to do what they did.

From that moment on, my thoughts were focused on creating situations so that people would want to stay with me and build something bigger. I understood that our dreams and plans need to be shared in such a way that others can decide if they would like to be part of it.

The fear of sharing our plans – for fear that they will steal our idea, for insecurity that we won't be able to fulfill them – is common. Sharing them with someone doesn't guarantee anything, but it does inspire them to embrace our project as their own.

Another lesson I learned during this phase, and which I only understood years later, was that gratitude is one of the noblest and most beautiful human feelings. Being grateful to the people who have helped you along the way is undoubtedly the right thing to do. Verbalizing, writing, telling and praising these people is also a virtuous attitude: it shows humility, the recognition that nobody can do anything alone, we always have help along the way and we do need to value the people who have reached out to us.

The other way around, however, is dangerous. Expecting gratitude from the people we help makes no sense. Firstly, because our evaluation of help can be – and probably will be – different from that of the person being helped. Secondly, we should do good to people because it enriches us, adds to us. It's how we should understand the world, as agents for improving the lives around us. When I do good to someone, I do it to myself.

The result of this practice is that we do good every day, on a much larger scale than those who only do it in their spare time. Altruistic thinking is replaced by a more selfish vision and, of course, we need to review the idea that selfishness is always linked to something negative. Wanting your own good is natural, and it doesn't mean not helping others, quite the opposite.

I decided to add more people to my dream, making jiu-jitsu their dream too, so that we could row together in the same direction, and I realize that I've really started to help more people.

The following years were a lot of work to implement and spread the new systematization throughout the group. The Alliance was large, as it was born that way, but extremely disorganized. Even though we had lost several renowned athletes, this had little impact on the number of schools, mostly non-competitors, and I was aware that the methodology was our product. We had to work hard to promote and develop it.

The future of a professional relationship between the Alliance Association and its members depended on transformation, on changing the hierarchical position of the martial art to a healthy commercial relationship. We needed to have the obligation to provide a structure that justified the price charged and brought value to those receiving the support. We were still a long way from that, but the methodology has arrived to be the backbone of this movement.

Since its foundation in 1993, member schools have only paid a monthly fee to help with the Alliance's basic organization. This model evolved very little, both in terms of values and the way this relationship was built. We had no room to invest in people or services.

Dedicated to my own gym, I intensified my private lessons, teaching ten to twelve workouts a day for a long time – starting at 7 a.m., with a short break to organize office things, pay bills, answer emails and make calls.

During competition training, I'd work with the class until 2pm, when I'd go for lunch. He returned at 4:30pm for more private lessons until 6pm. Then three more group classes.

This routine was adopted for almost a decade, when I proved beyond doubt that the well-applied methodology worked. My number of students multiplied in that time. It was a time of great focus in the gym, and it brought me some financial security.

My desire to dedicate myself grew more and more.

My decision to stop competing two years earlier had been a conscious one. My body was riddled with injuries, which was not unique to me as much as it was unanimous among all athletes in all sports who strive for high performance. And I could have continued competing if that had been the only reason.

The need to build a future through jiu-jitsu was my priority, and I felt it was getting late. At thirty-two, with my sights set on a successful academy, I visualized the possible paths where jiu-jitsu could take me. I drew up a clear plan for a natural transition, in which I dedicated myself to growing as a teacher.

A new challenge came my way when the director of TV Globo's affiliate network decided to hold an event called

"Perception and Leadership", and invited me to coordinate the jiu-jitsu activities. I researched everything I could to find material relating the concepts of the martial art to the business world. I only found a Judo book, which gave me a guide to prepare before the meeting. The idea was to put together a four-hour activity for a group of around a hundred people. If it would be challenging today, back then I didn't even know where to start.

I understood that it was a great opportunity for jiu-jitsu to reach another audience and for me, professionally, it could also be a way forward. I accepted, but explained that I'd never done a job like that before, and would dedicate myself to putting together something worthwhile for the event.

I divided the activities into a seminar, separated ten basic techniques – between defenses and attacks, all somehow connected – which made it easy for my students to understand the dynamics. Constant contact with the methodology helped me not to find it so difficult to create this sequence.

I then proposed some games, from relay to more specific answers, and divided them into groups. The class got involved and we managed to achieve one of the aims of the event – to get different areas, such as engineering and journalism, to help each other. At the end, I spoke about the concepts we had covered in the activities – team spirit, doing your best, respecting the rules, etc. It was a success and we repeated the event three more times in Foz do Iguaçu.

I started thinking about how I could turn this into a new product. I could bring jiu-jitsu to more people without them necessarily having to go to the gym. Even if I didn't win the student, it would certainly change many people's opinion of jiu-jitsu, which still suffered greatly from the distorted image of street gangs and brawlers in general.

I did some corporate events, but ended up turning my attention to the gym and the competition team. It was a long process. After all, you can't build a good team overnight.

At the time, Marcelinho was already receiving a lot of attention and more students, inspired by him and seeing that it was possible, began to dedicate themselves to training.

Little by little, the championships stopped hurting me as much as they did right after the "crack". I've never stopped going, and I've been to all the World Championships since they were created, but I didn't experience the real pleasure of attending from 2003 to 2006.

To find the light, you often just have to keep walking, doing what you can in the moment. And that's what I did. As uncomfortable as it was not to be the protagonist during those years, I was there. That made a difference.

As the 2006 World Championship approached, the process of building our team accelerated. We didn't have a great team, but the lower belts brought some results and the atmosphere at the championships was better.

A talent that could help us transform our history once again caught my eye on the mat that year. The featherweight category was contested between the favorite, Márcio Feitosa, and the newcomer to the finals, Rubens Charles, who defended Telles e Tererê (TT).

I asked Elan Santiago, during the final, who the fighter "killing" Feitosa was. "It's Cobrinha," he replied.

"Congratulations to him. Refined jiu-jitsu," was my comment.

Then he told me that Tererê, his cousin, wasn't well. He couldn't even be in the gym and give lessons. Elan believed that Cobrinha needed an opportunity.

***

The year 2007 was marked by changes, and there were two key figures. Our academies were improving in every respect. We were delivering better quality jiu-jitsu to our students and, although we still faced resistance from some members, we continued to evolve.

Improvement is a slow process, but the unwanted separation caused by the previous split has helped us to solidify the implementation of the method with fewer challenges.

Everything was going well, but our team, despite showing signs of improvement, still hadn't regained its full strength. To top it off, we were going to have to deal with a major casualty.

Marcelinho, who at that time was starting to travel a lot to seminars and fights, received an offer in the USA. Losing him at that moment was like taking away a fundamental piece of the team; he was our main reference. However, not allowing him to go could be more costly in the long run.

The team was becoming very decentralized, with champions coming from different places – Finland, New York, Atlanta, São Paulo and Rio de Janeiro. This diversity was crucial to the Alliance team's success.

As Marcelinho's proposal was to join our branch in New York, in a way it would strengthen our team there.

It wasn't easy to see him go, but after fulfilling his mission to keep the name of our school alive, he left a lasting mark on all the students who shared the mat with him over those almost five years.

In the middle of this process, I got a call from Cobrinha. We arranged a visit and, when he arrived at the academy, I didn't even suspect that I was standing in front of one of the main names in our team's history. When I asked him what had brought him to me, he said he needed a teacher.

Over the years, I have received many athletes who want to join a champion team, looking to enjoy success. This view often shows weakness or a lack of confidence in themselves, as if they wanted someone else to do for them what is necessary to become champions.

I prefer Cobrinha's approach, which demonstrates a life choice rather than a search for opportunity.

We continued talking, and he told me that he was a student of Tererê's and didn't intend to leave his academy. However, his teacher was ill and Cobrinha was worried about losing the *timing* for the peak of his career. It was Tererê's own suggestion, according to him, which made me very happy and surprised.

Although we were opponents in competitions, Tererê and I had a genuine connection and mutual affection. Receiving this nomination was proof of that. He was sending me his main athlete who, from that moment on, would be mine.

That very day, it wasn't hard to see that he had a unique talent on his hands. His way of training was contagious.

We gained intensity and marked the start of a new phase for us. With small details to adjust in his game, he trained tirelessly, improving his techniques even more.

This process brought a new method to our school, with the introduction of *drills* influenced by Cobrinha. The perfection of the movements and the exceptional commitment to training began to make a difference, and the competitions became a showcase, which we already knew would happen.

The overall level was growing, and the quiet domination in the featherweight category became comfortable enough to challenge him to compete at open weight. With several championships and impressive results for a featherweight, the following years only confirmed what I had already realized: one of the biggest names in the history of the sport was on our team.

Cobrinha had all the qualities a teacher could wish for in a pupil: extreme talent, unwavering dedication, loyalty, courage and tireless determination.

He joined the academy with the declaration that he was there for himself, without speaking on behalf of anyone or representing a specific group. However, his arrival opened doors for other athletes.

Although Cobrinha won the 2007 World Championship, Alliance came second. We're back in the title race.

CHAPTER 21

A jewel in my life

My gym shrank in size in 2005 and 2006, when I started sharing a room with Boxing to reduce the cost of rent. Those were difficult years and, as always, a lot of work. I managed to make ends meet thanks to my private lessons.

We gradually recovered and, with the development of the competition team, we ended up taking back the whole space. I had no problem negotiating with the academy, which was even happy.

At the age of 36, with everything back to normal, some money saved and a comfortable income, I felt it was time to get my own apartment and stop paying rent. So, when I passed a real estate development in the Brooklin neighborhood of São Paulo, I stopped to see it. It was more than I had saved and, even though I had to finance most of it, I decided to take a chance.

Dedication, study, training and insistence are recurring words, and jiu-jitsu was indeed providing me with a good life.

With the property bought, it was time to furnish it. To do this, I went to Marcus Ferreira, a friend with whom I used to take private lessons and who has become one of the leading professionals in the field in Brazil – founder of Decameron and Carbono – and asked for an architect. Carolina Rocco was the name I received.

I arrived at her office in the Jardins neighborhood and, as soon as she opened the door, I noticed how beautiful she was. We talked about my apartment, she gave me some ideas and I became more and more enchanted by her charm, her politeness and her competence. The meetings we arranged to discuss ideas after that became the best hours of my day.

On the very first visit to the building site, however, she realized that the apartment we had been shown was different from the one I had bought. A few days later, I found out that the realtor had made a mistake and, with all the properties sold, there was nothing left to do but cancel.

In order not to lose contact with a woman who was everything I had ever wanted, with the money returned and the gym in need of renovation, I took the opportunity. We had many more meetings. And finally, we started dating.

It was a new injection of happiness for me. The academy began to multiply in number, the competition team was winning many titles and my personal life was exactly where I had dreamed it would be.

Seventeen years have passed and our relationship has flourished. Today we have a delightful, true, loving marriage that is still going strong.

When we met, Carolina already had two children, Renan, 16, and Luiza, 7. Having children wasn't exactly in our plans, although it could become an issue in the future, but I had the experience of living with that sweet, fun girl and, without realizing it, I fell completely in love with her as I discovered her more and more.

Luiza allowed me to build such a true and loving relationship that today I have filled the gap of being a father.

Renan has become a friend and surfing companion after a few years of not being together as much. Our family is complete, happy and the most important thing in my life.

CHAPTER 22

Back to the top

On the back of our good results, more athletes were attracted to our academy and the teachers at Alliance schools around the world were motivated. The plan to take our team back to the top of the podium in ten years' time was about to be realized long before then.

With a cohesive, complete team full of talent, my dedication was almost total, and I continued to teach ten to twelve classes every day. When the competition class arrived, I was ready to train with everyone and lead by example. The group grew and improved.

We won the Pan American Championship for the first time. A few months later, the World Championships took place for the second time at the Long Beach University pyramid in California. It was a four-day event with the best in the world facing off in forty categories divided into four belts: blue, purple, brown and black.

At the end of the count – each champion scored nine points for the team; each runner-up, three; and the third-placed team, one – we were victorious for the third time, ten years after our first title, after being off the podium from 2002 to 2007.

I experienced an unparalleled sensation, which I didn't feel even when I was individual champion: a comeback, proof that I was right in what I believed, that working for the good of the team had paid off. Accomplished, although still a long way from my dream for the Alliance.

That title was very important, but it was just another *milestone* on our journey – or at least that's what I wanted.

We received congratulations from the Gracie de Humaitá and Barra. One of their members, however, said to me sarcastically: "You're really in a good phase. Enjoy it".

In fact, we had entered a good moment, with a very complete team across the board, but we wouldn't make the same mistakes as in the past: we would look after our champions differently, create opportunities for them to be happy by our side and, above all, I wouldn't relax. My plan was just beginning.

The phrase of unknown authorship "it's hard to be a champion, but it's much harder to stay a champion" is very true. As I've said before, when victory is the ultimate desire and goal, we tend to be stuck with only two outcomes: non-achievement, which frustrates, and achievement, which relaxes.

In my case as an athlete and as a coach, win or lose, I never relax. Winning is part of a much bigger process. The title, as important as it is, doesn't define anything. I've always worked hard to build a legacy, I want to do as much as I can in jiu-jitsu and for jiu-jitsu. No achievement will satisfy me and no defeat will discourage me, because those who win know the way. I keep training.

So, when I heard that debauched phrase from the fighter, I thought to myself, although I didn't say it: "you have no idea what I'm going to build so that this phase lasts until the Alliance is forever marked in the history of sport".

That title was no longer my goal: I would chase to become the greatest World Championship winner in history. I decided that this would be my time.

We started 2009 buoyed by the world title and with new challenges. The first was the European Championships in Lisbon, which we won for the first time. We went to the Pan in search of a second title, but we didn't manage it and came third. We won the Brasileiro and the World Championships, becoming four-time world champions. My focus at that time was to surpass Gracie Barra, with seven titles.

At that time, we already had some top athletes on our roster: Bruno Malfacine, Bernardo Faria, Cobrinha, Michael Langhi, Lucas Lepri, Marcelinho Garcia, Tarsis Humphreys, Sérgio Moraes, Leonardo Nogueira, Gabriel Goulart, Antônio Peinado, Henrique Rezende, among others.

My routine continued to be intense, with lots of private lessons, competition training and teaching students through the methodology. The gym grew exponentially, everything was going very well and I was happy.

In 2010, my first challenge was the European Championships. I had turned forty a few days earlier and had been competing in the masters, keeping up the pace and having fun doing what I loved best. I had a winning career in the category, losing only one fight in seven years.

Fighting as an adult is completely different. The techniques, pace, strength and psychological pressure are incomparable. As I trained every day with the best, there was certainly no other time to test myself. Each year got harder, but I was at peace in all aspects of life.

Getting out of my comfort zone has always been something I've seen as necessary in order to achieve extraordinary things. I signed up for the European Championships in the adult category, and stood next to my team, very excited to be able to experience that in the heavy weight black belt category. That year, my student Bernardo Faria was my partner in the category.

I won the first fight by a good margin of points. In the semi-final, I faced a Finn who had been our student there and was now one of the top athletes in Europe. I took him down and managed to finish him with a leg lock around four minutes into the fight.

In the final, to my delight, I would face the student who had won the other side of the bracket. Bernardo, in a gesture of great humility and generosity, gave me the victory without us having to fight. I admit that, although I was doing very well, I had little chance of beating him. He went on to become world champion months later.

With this title, I became the oldest champion of an IBJJF *Grand Slam*[38] tournament at adult black belt, a mark that still stands today.

Our team seemed unbeatable, but we still hadn't won all the championships in a single year – and that became the challenge for the team.

We made a bet: most of our athletes had tattoos – some too many in my opinion – but I had never had one. The chance of getting one was very low. They challenged me: if they won the European, Pan, Brazilian and World Championships that year, I would tattoo our symbol very large on my ribcage.

As we had already won the European Championship, all that was missing was the other three. We took it all and today I proudly wear our eagle on my skin. No team has ever achieved this feat. We repeated it three more times.

Since 2005, I had been living in a nice house in Morumbi, renting it. That year, the owner told me she wanted to sell it. I already loved the place and considered the opportunity. After negotiating, I managed to get a 40-month mortgage. The installments were high, but the gym was solid and I could afford it if I cut back a little. Just like the many titles I've accumulated throughout my career as a fighter and teacher, the victories in my personal life can largely be attributed to jiu-jitsu.

***

Every end of the season was a time of relaxation and preparation for our team. Trips and seminars made life very busy for our athletes, although I myself was more dedicated to the school. I received the news that the gym where we

38. It refers to the four main tournaments: European, Pan-American, Brazilian and World.

were located had been sold to the *Bodytech* group, and I knew it would be the end of the model I'd had until then – rent charged based on enrollment. With the new management, this would be impossible, even though they tried to reassure me in this respect.

The very next day I started looking for properties in the area to move to and, once again, I was forced out of my comfort zone. To leave inertia, you either have to force yourself or be forced. There is no such thing as stability; we need to seek constant growth and, to do so, take risks. If we don't, the world will do it for us – and that's always harder, because it doesn't allow us to prepare for change.

I then found a property two blocks away from the gym where I was currently 650 square meters, a large space by the standards of jiu-jitsu gyms at the time, but well suited to the *headquarter* of the best team in the world.

Certain that this would be another bold and necessary step, I rented and invested in the renovation at the same time as my own house was being finished. With cash flow low and expenses high – we would be paying for everything from maintenance and cleaning to electricity, gas and telephone bills – I entered a period of great savings.

We opened Alliance São Paulo in December 2010, a beautiful, spacious gym with three classrooms: one measuring 210 square meters, another exclusively for private lessons measuring 30 square meters and another for physical preparation measuring 40 square meters. We went back to the days when we had a place exclusively dedicated to jiu-jitsu.

The first month was complicated and we ended up in the red. Although all the students followed me, costs exceeded income – not by much, but enough to get my attention.

If I wanted to succeed, I needed someone who understood how to run this kind of business. It wasn't just about collecting fees and paying teachers' hourly rates. Running a gym involves many other issues that I simply didn't understand.

I remembered a friend who, many years before, had hired my services to teach at one of his facilities. Luís Amoroso had sold everything and was now working as a consultant in the *fitness* market. So I wanted to combine this knowledge with the jiu-jitsu methodology I had developed because I believed it would be a very successful combination. He agreed and we worked together for a few years.

I started to manage the business much more professionally, looking at indicators, student retention, sales conversion rates, etc., and this helped us to break records.

One of the first steps he took was to dismantle the fitness room, which was underused by the athletes and idle most of the time. The space became a tatami mat and we started offering more times, especially for beginners.

We broke through the 350-student barrier and suddenly we stagnated. We tried marketing campaigns, leafleting, internal campaigns, but nothing worked. Luís had taught me everything he could up to that point, and I needed more if I really wanted to leverage that successful model.

I had always understood that the *fitness* market was years ahead of jiu-jitsu and I had been looking for solutions there to apply to my own. Browsing the internet, I came across a post on Facebook that said "Gym full all year round", an event led by Junior Crocco, a digital marketing professional dedicated exclusively to the industry.

There was a lot of talk about ways to bring in new clients and trends, how digital marketing had the power to revolutionize the way everyone won students. I paid attention, but I found it very difficult to apply to jiu-jitsu.

Hiring management *software* was a differentiator. EVO, a product from the technology company W12, one of the sponsors of the event I was attending, was chosen.

I called Valério, founder of W12, and asked him how digital marketing really worked. He came to my office to talk about the best strategies. In the end, he advised me to start producing free content and hire RD Station, a digital marketing automation tool. Nowadays, this is common and basic; back then, it was revolutionary and unheard of in the martial arts market.

I learned everything I could while testing *lead* generation strategies. My first action was to distribute my PDF book for free to anyone who signed up to my ad. In 24 hours, more than four thousand *downloads* were made. I then held a prize draw for a kimono and got another five thousand registrations.

I communicated with the jiu-jitsu public directly via email, social media and my website. The next step was to attract them to my academy to become students. The strategy worked very well and we reached the magic number of 500 enrolments in less than a year of work.

A few months later, I was invited to speak at the biggest digital marketing event in Brazil, the RD Summit, and we became a success story for the platform.

Our team continued to break all records: we won practically every championship and competed against different teams in Europe, the USA and Brazil. The momentum continued, but I still wasn't satisfied.

We won the World Championships from 2008 to 2016, nine editions in a row, an unprecedented feat. They were all special, and each one has its own stories and particularities. In 2012, we equaled Gracie Barra's number of titles. In 2013, we surpassed it – which we continue to do year after year.

In 2015, on the way to our tenth world title and eighth in a row, we had a lot of confidence in our team.

Losing was always a possibility, but the milestone of ten world titles couldn't go unnoticed. Every year, our team wore a World Championship T-shirt and our fans took the same seats in the stands.

We didn't want to appear arrogant, but we couldn't help but celebrate an achievement of that size in style. I had the idea of making a double-sided one. On the outside, our logo and the name of the championship, as always. On the inside, a huge number 10.

If we lost, we'd leave without showing anyone our number. If we won, we'd turn the shirt around in the gym and the whole crowd would show the number of the ten-time champion.

We qualified six athletes for the black belt finals. Mathematically, it was enough for one to be champion.

Confirmation didn't take long. In the very first fight, the absolute final, Bernardo Faria's early victory was announced, after his opponent suffered an injury. In an exciting moment, the crowd took off their shirts and wore them inside out, showing the huge number 10. To top it off, Bernardo received double gold, also winning the super heavyweight.

We were applauded even by our opponents for being ten-time champions. The T-shirt tactic had worked perfectly and we were still going strong.

CHAPTER 23

The last fight

In 2012, I was having lunch with friends when I received a call from an international number. Guy Nievens, the English right-hand man of Shaikh Tahnoon of Abu Dhabi, was inviting me to do the *masters* superfight against Zé Mário Sperry at the following year's ADCC in China.

He was the only student on Carlson's team I hadn't fought yet, and one of the greatest jiu-jitsu and ADCC champions. It was a big challenge, so I jumped at the chance. I had almost a year to prepare, and just having a fight scheduled was enough to get me back to doing what I loved most. With the best team to train with, I started immediately.

I did the physical preparation – at the time, some of our athletes were using *crossfit*, and I thought it could be good, challenging and fun. I quickly got into shape, my weight dropped a lot and I got down to my competition number, around 92 kilos. Even without a weight division, I thought it was the best way to go.

Training intensified and an old shoulder injury began to bother me a lot. As injuries are part of any preparation and physiotherapy didn't solve it, I continued with painkillers.

I spent a fortnight in the USA with Cobrinha, who was also going to fight in China. It was great to be able to be a student rather than a trainer. We dedicated ourselves and I put myself through a routine that was totally out of my comfort zone. We usually started at 8.30am with six ten-minute *rounds*. Then *drills* on specific techniques or physical preparation. I would leave the gym at around 11.30am.

I returned to Brazil and continued training, incorporating the *drills* into my routine.

I invited Kenny Johnson, one of the best *wrestling* coaches in the USA, to help me. It was a very important move and I was able to learn a lot, since the sport is almost always decisive in the ADCC rules.

The fight was scheduled for October and, as it got closer, I worked harder in training. The routine was tiring me out and I couldn't wait for the date to arrive.

I booked my last period of practice in New York under Marcelinho Garcia, perhaps the greatest ADCC athlete – with four titles – and certainly the most exciting to watch fight. I arrived at the beginning of October for the last fifteen days of preparation. Two periods a day of just jiu-jitsu, and a lot of learning.

I stayed at Marcelinho and Tati's house, next to the gym in Chelsea. Everything was going well when, at the end of the last week, I started to feel discomfort in my lower back while I was sleeping.

I assumed it was just the result of hard training or the position I was sleeping in. I tried other positions, but by 4.30am the pain was excruciating and like nothing I'd ever felt before. I asked my hosts for help, and they rushed to call an ambulance. A urine test confirmed the presence of kidney stones. It was the only time I'd ever had them.

I returned to training unable to shake the feeling of fragility from my head. I kept a light pace, but being able to move without any pain was the most important thing at that moment.

I arrived in Beijing and, from the very first meal, I realized I was going to have a problem. I couldn't risk eating something different on the eve of a competition. Even outside the hotel, the options weren't the best. Many athletes had arranged to go sightseeing, including the Great Wall, but I did absolutely nothing but train and go back to my room, 100% focused, with no distractions.

I woke up on the day of the fight after a great night's sleep and, even though I followed the same ritual – a little mobility gymnastics to wake up my body – I felt more nervous than usual. I even went to the gym to watch the fights, but I realized that staying there for many hours would only increase my anxiety.

Having not competed for three years, the lack of rhythm gave me an adrenaline rush. At the appointed time, I went to warm up, but my body was sluggish, looking tired. I knew it was all emotional – I'd been through it hundreds of times – and when the fight started, everything would work out.

The fight began and I applied my initial strategy: the grip and an immediate *single leg*. He defended and we ended up off the mat, on the judges' table.

With the fight underway, there was no more anxiety and everything was back to normal as my master, Jacaré, had always taught me from a very young age. He used to say that we all get nervous, but the adrenaline would simply disappear once the fight started and I touched the kimono. There would be so many other things to concentrate on.

Practice is the best tool for confronting fear, the only way to remove this emotion from our thoughts. On the mat, we focus on grips, strikes and putting strategy into action.

In that stand-up fight, I felt a big difference in strength between us. He was 10 kilos heavier, and I realized it would be difficult to take him down. In the ADCC, pulling guard counts for one less point, but I had practiced this situation. I made an attack that I knew would be defended, and I managed to take the fight to the ground without characterizing it as a pull.

The match went on and on, with Zé Mário on top trying to pass the guard. He didn't expose himself too much, and I couldn't get into the positions I wanted, all of which he defended very well.

The match ended in regulation time, and we went to a five-minute *overtime*. We drew. In the second and final overtime, unable to think of another technique to use and with my opponent very well-positioned, we remained evenly matched. The judges decided in my opponent's favor.

As I've always done at the end of each fight – defeat or victory – I've analyzed my mistakes and successes, points for improvement and development. Regardless of the outcome, we come out of each fight different. What matters is figuring out what we're going to do with the new scenario we have in front of us.

That was my last fight, as I knew it would be. Maybe I'd been training wrong, maybe it had been too long and I'd lost too much weight. It was all just speculation – there wouldn't be a next fight and I had no way of correcting it.

I lived the experience, I fought against a great champion and, even though I didn't put in a dream performance, it wasn't bad at all. I could live with that. It was time to take care of my body.

When I got back to Brazil and the routine of the gym, my shoulder got a lot worse, and it bothered me not just when I was training, but in everyday life – like opening the car door, picking something up from the middle of the table and even when I was sleeping.

I was referred to one of the best shoulder specialists in Brazil, Dr. Benno Ejnisman, who diagnosed me, after analyzing my tests, with an advanced stage of arthrosis – only 30% cartilage in the shoulder joint. An arthroscopy for cleaning, a surgical procedure, was essential. It didn't solve the problem, but it did give me a few more years of comfort and mobility.

At the beginning of 2014, I had surgery. It was time for physiotherapy so I could get back to training. I used that time to think about my projects and get them off the ground.

CHAPTER 24

Alliance as a company

The Alliance as a team was founded in 1993, as we've already told you here, and a lot has happened since then. The people who were together and determined to set up the best team in the world have taken different paths, some setting up their own teams, competitors, others abandoning jiu-jitsu. Only three of us stuck to the original plan: Jacaré, Gigi and me.

As soon as I moved the gym to the new building in Vila Olímpia, I started to organize the branches a little better. To do this, I called in a student who was still a purple belt at the time to help me. Ricardo Caloi had just graduated in business administration and was passionate about jiu-jitsu, wanting to combine the two.

We started working on organizing the seminar agenda, the contracts with the branches, the methodology courses, etc. We needed to create an organization practically from scratch, which we did. After working on the units, I talked to Jacaré and Gigi about doing the same with theirs, as it would be very bad for the affiliates to use the brand differently and with different rules. They agreed.

In practice, it was very difficult to convince more than a hundred members to follow the new rules. They were all part of the team and loved it, but saw no need to change. I proved that the success of my academy was largely attributable to the processes created to manage the business, suggesting that they should follow suit.

The Alliance needed to take the same jiu-jitsu to all the schools. At the end of the day, everyone would benefit. I made it clear that I was there to help them.

Little by little, we broke down our resistance and learned to accept that the desired perfection was a long way off, that we were evolving, but we had a problem that seemed to be at the heart of the matter: three Alliances managed independently. We needed to bring everything together.

Talking to a student and friend from the financial market about how to develop the team as a business, he said that the first and most important action to take was to "combine the three umbrellas into one". The Alliance needed to function like a company, with a leader at the head of the business and unique rules for everyone. I was convinced that this was the way forward, but I needed to create arguments to explain the idea to the others.

The number of gyms we had was disproportionate between the three of us. However, when we talked about the brand, we should have equal weight and arguments would get us nowhere. We would each raise our own arguments. I had the biggest team and was responsible for the results of recent years. Jacaré was the master and was in the USA, where he had most of the gyms. Alexandre had opened up the European market.

I proposed a merger in a different way: one third of the shares for each, organizing Alliance jiu-jitsu Licenciamentos Ltda – the company that owns the brand and is responsible for all contracts with affiliates. In eighteen months, we would effectively evaluate the size of each and adjust the percentages accordingly. Everyone agreed.

I stayed on as executive and, together with Ricardo, we started working in a unified way. Some members tried to resist, but we were willing to lose some in order to organize the whole. We moved forward.

One of the first and most controversial measures was the decision to standardize all students in all schools, which generated a lot of discussion, especially since Gracie Barra had done this years before and lost several of its top athletes. I didn't think it was a good idea, and argued that it affected the student's freedom to wear whatever they wanted. In fact, it was also about the difficulty I would have to face, which I didn't feel ready for.

The fact is that the measure made perfect sense. Putting it into practice, I started with my gym, which had two complicating factors: it was the busiest and it brought together most of the competition team.

As the end of the year approached, I reinforced the stock and ran a promotion – students bought one and got two. The majority took advantage of this and we started the year with the gym fully uniformed.

Even with the rigidity of the rule, we didn't lose any students. We implemented a policy that would become extremely important for Alliance's business as a whole.

On the other hand, several of my athletes had kimono sponsorship and would certainly put up a lot of resistance. But I was determined and started talking about it. As expected, they got cold feet. I explained that in a few months it would be compulsory, we reinforced the idea with our suppliers so that we wouldn't run out of products, I told the students not to buy any more kimonos that weren't Alliance, because they wouldn't be able to wear them.

I spoke to them individually to explain the need and the plan, saying that we would improve the condition of all the gyms and that this would be important in the future.

Regarding the sponsors, I explained that they could wear whatever kimono they wanted at the championships, but the academy was not an exhibition for their sponsors and I didn't get anything for it. As students, they had to abide by the rules at school; as athletes and competitors, they could wear whatever they wanted.

The first renowned athlete who arrived without a uniform and was barred from training showed everyone that this was a serious matter, and that we would not accept exceptions. We never had any more problems and completed the uniforms in just a few months.

But the challenge was far from over. In my academy, standardization was successfully implemented, but not in the others. It would take time, but we would get there when the teachers realized that it was better this way, with a more organized and beautiful gym. Even the students' behaviour improved – uniforms don't exist for nothing, they symbolize belonging, order, cleanliness and everything that people look for in a martial art.

I knew we were on the right track and, little by little, we would break down all the objections.

Every step we took had as its vision the desire to do something great for the Alliance and for jiu-jitsu. My academy was doing very well, which gave me the comfort to devote more energy to organizing something that, although it had existed for a long time, was embryonic as a business.

We were in several countries and all we had to do was make everyone understand that the best competition team was also a solid and profitable business; all without losing the essence of jiu-jitsu. Even with a very low turnover, we were a global company.

We continued to do very well in the competitions and were so far ahead the other teams that, even with my energy focused on structuring the business, we were champions for the next two years, completing a run of nine consecutive World Championship and ending up with eleven men's and ten women's titles.

In 2017, we lost the World Championship to the Atos team, led by Professor André Galvão, who had been our main opponents for some time.

In every defeat, a series of experts and advisors always try to fill our heads with new ideas, and usually they've never done anything, they just criticize the work done. Because of the moment of fragility, we sometimes listen. In a way, I allowed this to happen. We suffered another defeat at the next World Championhsip.

We continued to make great strides in the organization of our company and I understood that I couldn't do everything at once: I couldn't lead the necessary renewal of our competition team. Our "golden knights", as we called the black belts, were nearing retirement, and the Alliance's best times were being left behind.

I had to accept that and move on, becoming as relevant to the company as I had been to the team. A new phase had begun, and I had to choose who would take my place.

Having created several champions, my main concern was to maintain a free environment and opportunities, because I wouldn't make the same mistake that, in my opinion, had been the real reason for the break-up almost fifteen years earlier.

The champions were always on the lookout for opportunities, and began to leave to set up their own gyms or to be invited by our affiliates to go and train in the USA. These were natural paths, which I understood and encouraged. Without realizing it, I didn't specifically prepare anyone to take my place.

With no time to take on classes, my quality and ability to keep up to date with new techniques and competitive strategies were compromised.

The choice of a successor had to be made quickly, but no one was ready for the job. Determination and reliability were requirements for the position, as well as representativeness, history and a sense of belonging. The ideal figure needed to have lived through our school's best moments on the mats, and clearly remember what it was like to be "led" so that he could build his own way of leading. I found that in Michael Langhi.

Mike was already the academy's head teacher, and he was taking on more and more responsibilities, especially with the competition team. Transitions aren't easy, which is why willpower and character need to be present so that we can get through the storms together. We had a lot of problems, and I wasn't always understood.

When dissolution isn't an option, you always find a way, and we did. Our team has started to be rebuilt.

CHAPTER 25

Making a living from jiu-jitsu

In 2017, after reaching five hundred students, I realized that I needed to share this not only with my Alliance affiliates, but with the entire jiu-jitsu community. It was urgent and necessary to abandon the mentality that proliferated in the 1990s, and which did not truly represent the essence of the art.

Gyms and teachers had to stop treating their students like martial disciples, and start understanding them as clients, who sought out and hired a service in the hope of improving their lives. This mentality was firmly entrenched in the minds of professionals, and I decided it would be my mission to break it down.

With the advent of the digital market and an easy channel of communication with the entire community, I developed a course called "Jiu-Jitsu Academy Management Course".

The face-to-face event at a hotel in São Paulo was publicized on the internet and we managed to fill the room with seventy people. It took almost four hours and I know it was a success.

I was pleased to have been able to give so many teachers a new vision. At the end, one of the students came up to me to congratulate me, saying that he had been very impressed, and that he hadn't expected so much relevant information for his business. However, he wasn't a jiu-jitsu teacher, just a practitioner, and was investing in a gym with his master.

We continued talking and he asked me if I knew *Empiricus*, a financial recommendations company that is very popular on the internet. Not only did I know them, but I also subscribed to their *newsletter*. This student gave me his business card and invited me for coffee to tell me how I could turn my course into a digital product. I kept Roberto Altenhofen's contact details in my wallet and, from the very first meeting, I decided to put his ideas into practice.

As well as recording all the lessons, the structure was divided into three pillars. The first is technical, about the importance of teaching methodology and the division of class levels (beginners, intermediate, advanced) and age groups. In addition, it deals with things that are practically non-existent in jiu-jitsu academies, such as setting up the class schedule. I proved that a good board could increase the maximum capacity of the number of students by up to 78%.

The second pillar, finance, covers how much to spend on rent, how to price tuition, how to pay staff and teachers, and even which accounting system to adopt.

Finally, the third pillar of the course is digital marketing, when I talk about the use of social networks, the logic of sharing free content to create authority and make customers want your product. I confess that I didn't like this point very much at first. Despite recognizing my value and knowing that my quality would sell itself, I found the term "marketer" pejorative. In one of my conversations with Beto, he commented: "If you don't do marketing, someone with much less quality will have a much louder and more powerful voice. You have a real mission to change people's lives through jiu-jitsu and if you allow anyone to speak in your place, you can't complain. You will have your share of the blame for the outcome."

It hit me like a bomb. Recognizing why, I completely changed my position; I started using the internet more and sharing as much free content as I could. The phrase "when the tide rises, all boats rise" became a mantra. The more I shared, the more people came up to me to thank me and say that they were changing their gyms and, consequently, their lives. It was the fuel I needed to keep going.

With five lessons recorded, I invited everyone to a free *workshop* – three meetings in the space of a week. We got thousands of subscribers and, at the last meeting, I announced the course of thirty lessons – even though I only had five ready. I told them they would have seven days to buy.

It was a success. I'd never done a launch like this before and, on the very first day, I sold five times as much as I did in person. The recordings were made by an industry professional in my office at the gym, in between classes. I even used a blackboard to write the content.

At the championships, the teachers thanked me and commented on the lessons, many asking when the next class would be. I managed to achieve what Beto had said – a ready-made product that could be sold several times over without having to record it again. And the audience reached was as wide as possible.

The challenge for online product launchers was to achieve the *slogan* created by Erico Rocha, a kind of launch wizard in Brazil: "make six in seven", i.e. make more than 100,000 reais (six figures) in seven days.

So, for the second launch, I did the publicity, generated the mailing list, invited people to the free *workshop* and followed the plan. I failed, but I came close.

I reached the "six out of seven" target on the third launch, but the most important thing was that hundreds of gyms were changing the way they saw jiu-jitsu. That was the great value.

The Alliance gyms that were closest to me improved and, consequently, my main business followed suit. Jiu-Jitsu has grown and I've tried to contribute even more to this growth in any way I can.

CHAPTER 26

Abu Dhabi

The capital of the United Arab Emirates has a special relationship with jiu-jitsu. My first experience in the country was in 1999, which I've already mentioned here, at an event organized by Shaikh Tahnoon bin Zayed, which became the biggest and most coveted *grappling* event[39] in the world. It all started much earlier, in the USA.

Shaikh Tahnoon, who had moved to California to study, discovered jiu-jitsu through the UFC and began training at the academy of Nelson Couto, a renowned athlete and teacher, and one of the first Brazilians to move there in the early 1990s.

At the end of the course and with plans to return to his country, he invited the teacher to move to Abu Dhabi to continue training him and develop the martial art in the region.

Some Brazilian teachers were invited to teach in the country, until one of the sheikh's sons, the first in command, was bitten by jiu-jitsu once and for all.

Seeing the positive transformation that the martial art had made in him, the sheikh made a decision that changed the world scenario for the sport: he made jiu-jitsu compulsory in all schools and military bases in the country. This required a lot of teachers, and the only place to get them was in Brazil.

39. Hand-to-hand fighting, such as Jiu-Jitsu, , Judo, *Wrestling*.

The great migration of black belts began: Brazilians chasing the dream of a comfortable life, of making a living from jiu-jitsu. The exponential growth stirred up the market and the IBJJF began to receive applications for diplomas from athletes who had been away from the sport for a long time, who saw the possibility of working with the martial art again.

Although this was beneficial for the fight, it also brought many problems, especially with teachers who weren't necessarily qualified to teach and who often didn't even speak English. Some dedicated themselves to taking advantage of the facilities rather than doing a good job for jiu-jitsu. Before long, more than six hundred teachers were in the country.

The sheikh remained passionate, training with the best athletes and teachers, whom he invited to spend a week with him at the palace. I had the honor of being invited a few times, and on the last occasion, the conversation was different.

Guy Nievens, his right-hand man, asked if I could help the jiu-jitsu project as a whole, pointing out that my name was first on the list in an attempt to organize and structure the project.

I undertook to think of a way to help, and we decided that it would be important to visit Abu Dhabi to understand the idea from the inside. During that week of training with the Shaikh, I had another goal and another professional challenge. I was excited.

We talked about the problems he identified and I gave my *input* on how I thought we could work towards unifying the way jiu-jitsu was taught. As I'd already been through this experience with the implementation of the methodology at Alliance, I knew that even though it wasn't an easy job, it was possible.

I took the ideas to the project commander, Colonel Abdul Manan, with whom I met a few times during the week and left the country with a deal practically done.

Back in Brazil, there was a lot to sort out. The first was Carolina, who didn't like the idea of us moving to Abu Dhabi at all.

Then I had to think about how to continue developing the Alliance plan even from afar. These were manageable issues, especially with the attractive financial proposal – US$ 1,200,000.00 a year plus benefits such as housing and tickets to Brazil three times a year. In my mind, the offer was incredible.

The contract arrived stipulating a different amount from what had been agreed and, assuming it was a typo, I contacted them. To my surprise, the colonel had actually understood that the payment would be calculated in *dirham*, not dollars. For that amount, I didn't agree to move my whole life to Abu Dhabi.

A few weeks passed and I received a message inviting me to spend a month in Abu Dhabi consulting on an ongoing project. They paid my price and went.

For the first fortnight, I only attended the classes of the competition team – led by one of my students, Henrique Rezende, and two other friends, Michel Maia and Alex Negão. I was very well received, but they didn't invite me to visit the Palms Sports headquarters and get a better understanding of the project's structure. That didn't happen until the third week, when I actually had a schedule of meetings with the company's CEO, Fouad Darwish, and was able to make my recommendations about what I had seen and what could be improved.

It was a rich experience, although not as rich as it would have been if I'd really been in charge of the technical and methodological side.

I learned a lot and, in a way, made my contribution so that jiu-jitsu could take a better and more organized course there. To this day, from what I can follow through friends who are part of the project, they still haven't managed to establish a uniform working methodology. Even so, jiu-jitsu is part of the country's culture, which in itself is a huge achievement.

I believe that the sheikh understood the problem and pointed me in the direction of the solution, which we both agreed was the best way forward, of having someone who was representative of the group of teachers so that a single form of teaching could be established. This would allow us not only to see the technical progress of the students, but also to measure the quality of the content taught by the teachers.

For the colonel, who was all-powerful in the project and decided the direction and "how to do it" – even though he didn't know jiu-jitsu in depth – it wasn't interesting to have someone like me in that position, even more so directly appointed by the sheikh. Hence the whole strategy of interpreting the contract differently and taking me to a consultancy.

The fact is that everything has remained as it was, and to date we haven't seen any significant change in the direction of delivering a more cohesive and quality jiu-jitsu in Abu Dhabi.

CHAPTER 27

Alliance: single focus

After Abu Dhabi, my focus once again became the growth of the Alliance. The demands on bringing support to our affiliates increased and, alone, I and Ricardo Caloi, who had moved to Florianópolis, were not able to do the job.

Torn between academia and the Association, I felt we had to take another leap in quality. We needed people. Ricardo is married to Camila, a *designer* who was looking to reframe her work. She thought she'd help us at the Alliance, and it would be great to have a female eye on our team. As well as bringing a skill we'd never had before, it was someone who could take care of our brand image.

Even though it was a great plan, I had to convince them to move to São Paulo, because working remotely didn't appeal to me and I didn't think we could get the best out of being apart. Discussing ideas was essential at this stage.

We started working together. The next step was to move to another office, as mine couldn't handle the growth we were planning.

***

One day, Florian Bartunek contacted me with a proposal to invest in Alliance. He, one of Brazil's biggest investors, had been following my work for many years and giving me valuable tips on studies, books, courses and business over our occasional coffees. It was informal mentoring, which has always been of great value to me.

At the time, I had just carried out a *valuation* study of Alliance, because I wanted to understand the possibilities that lay ahead. Although we were still a relatively small company in terms of turnover, we had some interesting characteristics, such as a significant part of our revenue in dollars, capillarity in around thirty countries and a sports and health segment that aimed to develop people in search of virtues; things that few businesses managed to bring together.

We set up a meeting a few weeks later, and I presented the valuation that I felt was fair for the company at the time. Florian agreed, but said he would like three more people to share the purchase of 10% of the business with him.

For him, it's not very difficult to get partners and, within a week, three new interested parties of the highest caliber came forward: Gilberto Sayão, Fábio Nazari and Maurício Sirotsky. That was a *dream team* of partners, no doubt about it.

We went deeper into the negotiations in terms of governance and responsibilities, all quite new to me, although I had always read a lot about the subject. At one point, I came across a clause that made me uncomfortable – an "exit *put*" that basically said that, in seven years, investors could sell their shares, obliging the company to buy them at a certain valuation multiple. Even though I didn't really understand it, it felt like a loan with a repayment date.

I tried to deepen my understanding, as I didn't want to miss out on the opportunity to have such great partners who would certainly help me a lot in the process of developing the business, but my discomfort continued. It was, in fact, customary in the market for investment funds to program an exit at a profit, but that still sounded like debt to me.

I tried to negotiate the exclusion of the clause, but was unsuccessful and declined the offer. It was a very difficult decision, but I felt it was the right one. I thanked him, explained my reasons and we decided not to close the deal. We're still good friends and, in a way, I have advisors who indirectly help Alliance to grow.

During the meetings, we discussed a lot about the plans and what to do with the money we would receive – where to invest, hiring staff, organizing the company, etc. These were priceless lessons with some of the brightest minds in the market.

I knew what to do, but I wasn't sure I could afford it.

A few months earlier, a student from San Diego had proposed buying a piece of the gym as an investment, because he wanted to have jiu-jitsu in his life forever. Bobby Armijo wanted to do more for the sport and the Alliance, and was looking for new opportunities. He came to Brazil often, had become a friend and so I offered him the same deal I had just turned down, albeit without the exit clause. He agreed on the spot and, in less than two months, we had a new partner in Alliance, as well as the cash to begin the structuring I felt was necessary.

There is a fable about a Chinese farmer who had a young son and a horse. One day, he received news that the horse had disappeared. The animal was responsible for transportation, as well as helping to work the land. Without it, the farmer couldn't feed his family. Many lamented the farmer's "misfortune", and he replied: "Is it really a misfortune?"

The horse returned a few days later, bringing with it two more animals. Now the farmer had three and people rushed to congratulate him on his great "luck". "Is it?" replied the man.

The next day, happy and excited, his son went out riding, fell and broke both his legs. Again, people pointed out his "bad luck". "Is it really bad luck?" the farmer asked. A week later, the army arrived at the farm to summon all the young men to war. His son was spared because of his injury.

Good things can happen on journeys that initially seem bad. The truth is that we'll only find out along the way. We face new challenges and opportunities and, if we waste energy categorizing, we'll miss other chances. Whenever we feel sorry for ourselves, we look back at what happened and not forward to the new steps to be taken.

In a fight, we try to do something that our opponent doesn't want to allow us to do. It's a contest between totally antagonistic wills. In a way, it forces us to be in the present all the time, looking at possible scenarios. When we fall into a trap and regret it, we become vulnerable. In a split second, it can strike us and win the fight, all while we're thinking about something we can't fix.

This logic must be replicated in life at all times. When we have a problem or suffer a defeat, we need to be pragmatic. We shouldn't waste a single second regretting or making excuses for what happened; it doesn't matter and has no power to help you. The only thing that can get us out of the problem is to think of the best possible move from the situation.

A bad event can require much more than just one action. Sometimes, it requires a sequence of right actions. At other times, it takes much longer than we would like to clear the way. I don't think it's very effective to despair or simply sit back and hope that it will happen. We need to work on the best we can do, at the very moment we are.

In a fighting context, when your opponent has control of your back and one arm around your neck – just one move away from achieving a victorious choke – a quick look back at your techniques will make you conclude that you've made consecutive mistakes, that you've made the wrong decisions. Perhaps, while you're thinking about it, your opponent will use the other arm and define the fight.

In a difficult position, whether or not it's the result of a succession of mistakes, it's practically ineffective to think about it while deciding on the next move.

In the hypothetical situation above, if you just concentrate on not being strangled, you might be able to avoid it. From then on, you may be able to move away from the blow and the dominance imposed by your opponent. By following the strategy with every move, things will invariably get better and, when you least expect it, you'll be in a favorable situation, and even on the verge of winning the fight.

This is, in my opinion, one of the most important concepts in dealing with problems. Being focused on our ability to adapt and not getting too attached to what we might lose at any moment means that we are always prepared to react in the best way when undesirable things happen. The limit of this thinking lies in the stoic concept *memento mori* – reflecting on death, being aware that it will come to all of us at any moment without warning – which makes us force ourselves to act without wasting time, not to procrastinate our tasks, not to pass up the opportunity to tell people how important they are, and definitely to live in the present and be ready to act in any situation that comes our way.

Adaptability requires us to look ahead, to trust that we will find our way out and that this will lead us to new achievements and challenges.

Looking forward is at the heart of logotherapy, a therapeutic doctrine that, in a way, opposes psychoanalysis – or, as some say, the third Viennese school of psychotherapy.

In his best-seller *Man's Search for Meaning*, Austrian author Viktor Frankl portrays the importance of solving problems by looking at the things to be done, leaving aside vicious circles and feedback mechanisms which, according to him, are largely responsible for creating neuroses, as well as being ineffective in actually solving problems.

The opposite, in other words, looking back and seeking justifications is directly linked to victimization, the search for a culprit – "anyone but me" – and we tend to believe that the world is conspiring against us, that this isn't fair. "My God, why me?" or "Why me?"

Our actions have consequences, as do our ideas, and we need to be ready to pay the price for them, which has nothing to do with justice. This concept means the desire for things to be as we see fit and right, and is totally detached from the reality of the world.

Thomas Sowell, in *The Quest for Cosmic Justice,* explains the difficulty that many people find between what is desirable and what is possible and real. He explains that there is no doubt that the world of cosmic justice is infinitely better than that of traditional justice. However, it is one thing to protest against fate – and no one should confuse this with a serious criticism of existing society – and another to use it as a basis for building something better.

Throughout this book, I've recounted some defeats and difficulties that led me down paths that weren't in my plans. They were hidden opportunities that, without all the setbacks, I wouldn't have experienced. I've always looked at life from the positive side, and jiu-jitsu taught me how to find ways out.

Bobby joined our firm through one of those unforeseen paths and since then he has been a great friend and advisor, practically a faithful thermometer of the North American market.

The USA has great potential for the growth of our company, and we have forged a deep friendship over these five years. "All's well that ends well" has been confirmed: I missed out on an incredible opportunity for a partnership with four brilliant minds, I've continued to have them all as friends and partners, and I've gained a loyal, collaborative and competent partner.

Thinking of Alliance as a company was something I had been doing amateurishly for a long time. My relationship with the other founders, Jacaré and Gigi, went far beyond a simple partnership – we had always been together, and our friendship always gave me the peace of mind to be at the forefront and defend our interests in the best way. With the arrival of a new partner, who believed in our growth potential, we took on new responsibilities and commitments.

At the age of forty-nine, my body was already feeling the passage of time. It had been many years of training, often without respecting limits – as happens with high-performance sports – and the act of teaching had begun to bother me.

The shoulder injury and the discomfort I had started to feel in my hip forced me to realize that my life on the mats wouldn't be much longer. Even though I knew it was the natural course and had prepared myself – a successful academy with a team of very qualified teachers – two things came to mind. Firstly, my teachers would want to go their own way. Secondly, I needed to dedicate myself completely to the Alliance Association.

CHAPTER 28

Choosing a successor

During the golden years of our team, between 2008 and 2016, I had under my command the best jiu-jitsu team in history, with nine consecutive World Titles, as well as Brazilian, Pan-American and European titles. We trained dozens of world champions to black belt, and many of them naturally started looking for their place in the job market.

Everyone was building their careers and I saw this with good eyes, because that was the plan: to turn the Alliance into a platform of opportunities for those who wanted to make a living from jiu-jitsu.

As part of this expansion movement, Michael Langhi was invited to be the *head coach* of our Orlando academy in Florida in 2012, and he called another of the team's stars, Bruno Malfacine, to join him.

That generation of players was seeing the end of their competitive lives and putting themselves on the market, fuel for all those who would follow. It's a fact that our team missed them, and it's almost impossible to replace such brilliant players quickly.

Excited about Michael's arrival, the owner of the branch announced on the internet the arrival of a new teacher, who would take over the classes immediately after the small renovation that was underway. Mike arrived in the city to acclimatize, organize his accommodation and apply for a work visa. With everything organized, his wife went to meet him to start their new life together, but US immigration prevented their entry.

Michael returned to Brazil and was denied a work visa, missing out on the World Championships the following year. It was a difficult time for one of our team's greatest champions.

As the saying goes, "when one door closes, others open". While I was thinking about my successor, I saw Michael's return as a great opportunity to keep a star in my gym. He was always one of the most committed athletes I've ever dealt with – the first to arrive and the last to leave – he never complained of tiredness and always did what had to be done. He fought and won every possible championship, becoming one of the greatest exponents not only of our team, but of all jiu-jitsu.

I jumped at the chance to make him see the situation in a better light and, at the same time, guarantee the continuity of my work with the team at the academy.

Teachers have a different mission from athletes, but we would have enough time to prepare him to take over. I offered him a share in the results, and he became the school's main teacher, freeing up my schedule for administration.

A while later, I was faced with the need for total dedication to the association, and decided it was time to offer Michael control of the gym. As successful as he was, he lacked the funds to buy a profitable business like Alliance SP.

So we negotiated a form of payment in installments over a few years. I was freed from my academy duties – at least directly – and could devote myself to organizing the branches and breaking new ground for Alliance.

Again, athlete and teacher are very different positions from manager. We also had to lead the competition team, which involved a huge emotional component. Even though

Michael was one of the greatest champions to have been trained there, the athletes saw him much more as an experienced teammate than as the leader of the group. It was an emotionally difficult time for everyone, but things soon flowed better.

Many people find it difficult to delegate tasks, especially in the case of succession. We have to bear in mind that we can't do everything ourselves and accept the differences in the way things are done – we can even provide guidance, but the new owner of the role needs to learn how to deal with difficulties and problems. Otherwise, we won't have leaders helping us, let alone successors.

And that brings us to one conclusion: a successor needs to be aligned with the vision and purpose of the business, and share the same moral and ethical values. I believe that everything else is secondary and can be learned.

I chose Michael Langhi with that in mind. Of course, his technical quality and commitment have always been there, but on their own they wouldn't have put him in this position. Allied to these characteristics, his loyalty to everything the Alliance stands for and his character were decisive in my choice.

△

CHAPTER 29

The bomb of 2020

The year began and we were full of plans. We moved to a new office, increased our team to better serve our members, started to provide regional services for members in Brazil, the USA, Canada, Europe and Asia, as well as a brand and marketing department. We were ready to put the plan into practice, and with money in the till because of Bobby's arrival.

Finally, there were rumors that our school in China would have to close for two weeks in an attempt to contain the spread of a virus. As the information coming from there is always murky and not very reliable, we were on alert, but we didn't take any action.

The problems kept coming – schools in Europe, Oceania, the USA and Brazil – and before long we were all closed.

All the information coming in was very superficial, and no one knew for sure what to do. The "herd effect" led everyone to believe that a two-week *lockdown* would control the spread of the virus and that, little by little, we could return to normal. "Two weeks," said the authorities. Many panicked and I had to act to reassure them.

I don't remember if I called for advice or if Florian Bartunek himself contacted me to find out how I was doing, but the fact is that once again I was enlightened by the advice of this great friend, who offered me access to five *masterclasses* held by Harvard for a group of entrepreneurs and students in order to discuss and find strategies for facing the unknown. I attended all of them with great interest and began to better understand the scenario that lay ahead of us.

Anticipating the imponderable is an art that always needs to be practiced. Once again, I turned to the teachings of jiu-jitsu: anticipating every move the opponent makes, even those with different characteristics in terms of weight, speed, aggressiveness, flexibility, etc. To prepare for the unknown is to become adaptable, and this is perhaps one of the best qualities to develop in order to navigate the future – which is, by definition, uncertain.

It's not a question of trying to guess what's coming, but of preparing for it. That's what keeps us busy in the present: doing what we can to evolve. Holding on to attempts to control the inevitable feeds the evil of anxiety. Doing what we can is the best medicine.

The first lesson I took away from the classes was that the problem was not unique to anyone – everyone was in the same boat and, as in any crisis, some would sail well and others would not. In a way, I was confident and understood that I needed to take care of my competition team first.

To guide the gyms on how to proceed, I helped Michael deal with ours. First there were the teachers, who would not be able to teach and, consequently, would have no income. The two weeks foreseen by the competent authorities stretched on indefinitely, but we announced that their salaries would be maintained.

Then we explained to the students what we were going to do and we experienced a great victory in the pandemic. The overwhelming majority of them supported our plan and kept paying the fees, showing that jiu-jitsu is much more than just a physical activity.

While other gyms were closing, totally without income due to the high level of drop-outs, our cancellation rate was close to 30%, even though most of the students were also financially affected in their businesses.

We created a schedule of daily meetings with all the affiliates in five different regions of the world to talk about the measures, create routines for online classes, build an organized and safe feedback protocol – according to what we knew at the time, respecting distance and fixed pairs during classes.

We discussed the policies of the different countries and, by the end of the lockdown period, we had a much more cohesive team of subsidiaries. Everyone who took part in the meetings was able to keep their business going, and even more motivated to do better.

Seeing the students supporting the academies all over the world was a very pleasant surprise, and reinforced my purpose of serving them better and better through our schools. My mission was more alive than ever.

On the other hand, I realized that we needed to pay back the four months of monthly fees that we had received without providing services, and so we created vouchers that could be used for products and services. In just over a year after returning to activity, we had already returned almost everything. We have come through the test of the pandemic even stronger.

On the personal side, once we were forced to stay at home, there was little we could do. I saw the opportunity to dedicate myself even more to my studies and made a commitment to read religiously for at least an hour a day. I had been wanting to develop the habit for a long time, and I succeeded. I started with an hour and increased it to two books a week.

I also kept up an hour-long exercise routine – I have a small gym at home where my family does their activities.

Reading Nassim Taleb's *The Black Swan*, I came across reflections on the media and how we are manipulated. He compares the time wasted in front of the TV, newspapers and even the radio, highlighting how damaging this is, since we only consume news filtered by group interests – not necessarily, not to say almost never, dedicated to the truth. I've always made a point of being "informed". These days, I realize I should say "manipulated".

The question raised by Taleb is simple: "Who will learn more: a person who watches two hours of news a day or someone who exchanges those hours for reading great works of literature?" Two hours a day, at his rate, would mean a hundred books a year. That hit me like a bomb, and I decided to change immediately. Since then, I've never watched the news on TV again.

Daily reading is undoubtedly the object of constant transformation in my life. I started with Jordan Peterson, who is still little known to most Brazilians, and he opened up another arsenal of writers. Alexander Soljenítsin, who sparked my interest in Russian authors, Dostoyevsky, Tolstoy, Gogol and the whole history of the country since the Romanov dynasty.

My world is getting bigger, along with the certainty that I'll never know enough – another learning from jiu-jitsu.

Curiosity about the pandemic, and how to deal with something so unusual, led me to John M. Barry's *The Great Influenza*. The book is an account of the disease that affected a huge part of the population at the end of the First World War. The devastation hit mainly young men and appeared in military training camps in Kansas in the USA, where soldiers were being prepared. In this episode, there was a strong manipulation of the media to hide the disease – and the same happened in almost all European countries – in order to minimize the problem and keep the morale of the troops high.

As Spain was not involved in the conflict and did not control the media to hide the cases, many believe that it was the place most affected – hence the name "Spanish flu", a slight manipulation that makes us understand the danger of the power of those who hold the narrative.

The book goes on to describe the measures taken by governments, totally lost and ineffective, creating *lockdowns* and border closures in an attempt to contain the virus, all of which failed. The use of masks was not exclusive to our times either, adopted over a hundred years ago, when two cycles of the virus hit Europe hard, killing thousands of people in one of the deadliest pandemics of modern times.

Science has rushed to try to find an antidote, and disputes between doctors with different lines of thought have not reached a conclusion on the cause or even the pathogen responsible for the disease – all very similar to what we are experiencing in 2020.

I began to question the measures taken arbitrarily and without the slightest sensitivity towards the people, such as preventing people from working, the source of their livelihood. In the name of science, political interests spoke louder, the quest for power and control took hold of leaders all over the world, information about a disease with a low mortality rate led to panic throughout society.

Nothing made sense, but the arguments were difficult, generating accusations of a lack of empathy for others, especially the elderly.

After a few months and considerable damage to commerce, we're back to socializing in restaurants and gyms – with the obligatory use of masks.

The open hypocrisy, as well as the weakness of the people in defending themselves against abuses of their individual freedoms, was reflected in the rules: in restaurants, we could go without masks while sitting down, but we had to put them on to go to the toilet. It was like saying that the virus only affects those who are standing.

Like this example, many others have been observed. How could we not challenge such ludicrous measures? How could we believe absolutely everything that the newspapers and politicians, defended or attacked by the media, told us?

People became "mask inspectors" and inflated themselves as if they were the only virtuous people in the world. They were manipulated in a way we had never witnessed before.

This phase was far from over. Vaccines were finally launched on the market, in a major global effort coordinated by Big Pharma, with business figures serving as poster boys for what would be the only way to return to normality.

Political and scientific disputes took center stage, although the mainstream media only reported the arguments of one group's interests, silencing and canceling out any voice that disagreed with the imposed narrative or that merely questioned its effectiveness and side effects, all in the name of science.

This bypassed a basic scientific principle: putting the theory under public scrutiny. The doctors who objected were erased from the annals, lost any space in the press and blocked on their social networks.

Censorship has been reborn in many places around the world, including Brazil.

CHAPTER 30

Coral band

With the respite given by the pandemic at the end of 2020, even with many restrictions, life began to return to normal.

On October 23rd of the following year, I completed thirty-one years as a black belt. And it was my last, because I received the symbolic red and black, 7th degree, known as the choir belt. This is the beginning of the master phase, which continues for another seven years until the red and white belt, 8th degree. Then another nine years to the last, the red belt, 9th degree. The 10th degree is reserved only for the founders of Brazilian Jiu-Jitsu, the five Gracie brothers – Carlos, Oswaldo, George, Gastão and Hélio.

I always knew that if I stayed alive and healthy, it would only be a matter of time before I reached these levels. As I didn't intend to give up martial arts, I waited without anxiety.

The diploma is awarded by the IBJJF and I received it at the office. The ritual on the mat was performed with my student, Michael Langhi, who took on the honor of tying the new belt around my waist.

The coral belt, like all the others, doesn't change who you are or how much you need to keep studying and learning, even though I made an important decision with its arrival.

Looking after Alliance, I ended up spending more time in the office than on the mats. Michael had already taken over the leadership of the academy, and we understood that, from that moment on, I should no longer refer students to black belts, who were then graded by Michael as my mine. My list stopped at 139, all remembered and listed at the end of this book.

I received a beautiful tribute from the office staff, who organized a dinner with students, friends and family to celebrate this new degree and mark another achievement in my career.

CHAPTER 31

Making the most of downtime

A second wave of the pandemic forced us to close the gym again. This time, I took the opportunity to take care of my body. My shoulder, operated on in 2014, was showing signs of pain. So I made another appointment with Dr. Benno, when I discovered that the remaining cartilage had disappeared. A new operation was necessary – and not an arthroscopy, but an open operation with the aim of placing a piece of titanium to cover the head of the humerus so that I could regain movement of the joint.

The surgery was a success, but the recovery wasn't very easy, as we expected from a procedure of this size. The injury was many years old and the muscles were somewhat messed up in their functions. Only a lot of discipline made me functional again.

With my shoulder 70% recovered, it was time for my hip, which had been bothering me for a long time. Again I spoke to Dr. Benno, who referred me to another specialist, Dr. Roberto Dantas.

This surgery was much more frightening, meaning cutting off the head of the femur, inserting a titanium and porcelain rod, which would fit into another piece fixed in place of the acetabulum – a total prosthesis. I didn't know anyone who had returned to training after the intervention, but there were no options left: my quality of life had diminished considerably, to the point where even walking became a major nuisance.

It was another problem I had to face, but I put it in my head that I would be able to train again without any limitations. Six months after the shoulder surgery, I was admitted to the Albert Einstein Hospital again.

When I woke up from the procedure, which ensured that the intramedullary nail fitted perfectly into my femur, I felt like I had fought a bear; literally wounded. Within 24 hours, we started physiotherapy. Very motivated, I began to recover, went home and continued to improve a little every day.

The exercises increased. I started cycling ten days after the surgery and intensified until, sixty days later, the physiotherapist agreed that I should return to jiu-jitsu.

I invited one of my best teachers from the gym to help. Caio Rigante came to my house twice a week for two months so that I could learn the techniques and movements. I progressed a lot and, after four months, the worst was over and I was back in the gym.

I lived with some limitations for a while longer – I tried to do the movements as before – and little by little I felt fully recovered. Overcoming the uncertainty about whether or not to return to jiu-jitsu, I was very excited, happy and feeling much better than a few years earlier, when I had to live with a lot of pain.

Today, I still wonder if all the moves I made to get out of the gym were influenced by that phase when I stopped believing in my body's recovery. As we get older, we tend to accept the worst performances. That's natural. But we don't realize how good we could be if we simply didn't accept it.

Regardless of age, if we do our utmost for ourselves, take care of our bodies through intense exercise, adopt a clean diet, pay attention to sleep and keep our minds always in the process of learning, our lives will have more quality. The recipe doesn't sound complicated, but the truth is that many people don't discipline themselves to do it.

All these attitudes are directly linked. A good amount of intense exercise, preferably with some degree of competitiveness, leads to responsibility for the main energy fuel – your diet. By getting these two things right, your sleep will invariably be much better and your health will reach optimum levels.

During my adult life, I've come to feel better, more willing and healthier compared to other times when I was younger, all because I've become more disciplined about what's really important for my health. Stopping doing the right thing because of the excuse "I'm old" seems to me to be the recipe for an unproductive and increasingly difficult life, which will soon lead to total dependence on other people and poor quality. Therefore, we must always do the best we can until thought dominates every sphere of our lives.

Don't seek the easy, deal with sacrifice and challenge, this will make you live a constantly evolving life.

CHAPTER 32

A new phase

We came out of the pandemic with the conviction that we all need a strength like jiu-jitsu even more. I was shocked by people's fragility and insecurity, and I know that the practice can help them become safer, more confident and more courageous. The mission to transform lives remained firm and increasingly clear in my mind.

Jiu-Jitsu has always been seen as an efficient martial art, which is why it has attracted millions of people to its mats. However, I began to question what kept people in the practice for so long.

There was certainly something more to be explored in the field of communication – how we "sold" jiu-jitsu – and if we really wanted to create an impact on society, we would need to reach a new layer, those who were unaware of the benefits it brings to their lives.

Of course, "self-defense" is a differentiator. After just a few months of training, students already feel able to defend themselves. Instead of stopping, many continue. The training can be hard and difficult, but those who persist love it. It's not hard to see their lives really change, whether it's their physical appearance – which is always healthier – or their posture and energy.

Looking for answers during the pandemic, I did something I had long been curious about: a course at Harvard. I asked Florian Bartunek for a recommendation, and he said "*Disruptive strategy*".

Still unsure whether I could handle the dynamics and keep up with the classes, I enrolled. It was an intense eight weeks of study and a very worthwhile experience, with many insights, including strategies that I had already been applying in my business.

I discovered a marketing classroom platform, *Section 4*, led by professor Scott Galloway from New York University (NYU), and enrolled in a course called "*Brand strategy*".

I invited Camila, our marketing director, to do it together. It was a 21-day *sprint*, in which we took ease our pain on how to communicate the Alliance and jiu-jitsu not only to our direct clients (the affiliates) but also to the student at the end.

We studied the possibilities for presenting the brand and communicating jiu-jitsu. At the end, we submitted a complete project on the problem and the ways to solve it. Although the exercise itself was very worthwhile, Camila presented a piece of work that was dense in content and beautiful graphically. We then signed up for what would be the last master class with Professor Scott Galloway.

We didn't know the dynamics. He summarized the entire course and analyzed the three best projects. Among the thousand submitted, to our surprise, ours was there, shared on the screen, and the martial art displayed as an outstanding business on one of the best and most respected marketing platforms in the world.

I've experienced this sense of pride in other courses and classes I've taken at Harvard, where I've always made a point of bringing the Alliance and our business model up for discussion.

I began to realize that what I had always believed was getting closer to becoming a reality. It wasn't time to relax; on the contrary, we needed more commitment, and the key was communication.

I learned Jiu-Jitsu from Jacaré who, in his explanations, always used analogies so that we could better understand the technique and especially what is invisible – things like *timing* and connections that the movement would provide. Using something familiar as a reference so that our interlocutor has a better understanding is the most efficient form of communication.

Jiu-Jitsu, in order to become as big as I had always dreamed, needed to advance and become not only an efficient martial art – without which nothing would make sense – but a tool for personal development, in which the answers to a virtuous life can be found.

How to get this across to people who have never practiced jiu-jitsu? How to get them to experience some of these benefits? The habit of reading brought me the answers.

Philosophy, and the attempts to understand the human being, immediately led me to make connections with what we experienced in the fight, how the practice of Jiu-Jitsu reinforced these concepts, and I began to bring this to the students. My aim was to make them realize what training represented in their lives outside the mats.

I received hundreds of reports about how it made sense – focusing on what is possible is essential both for practicing jiu-jitsu and for solving problems in life. Consistency shows results over time, it's one of the many fundamental concepts for living a good life.

My mission to bring jiu-jitsu to more people was renewed. Like many times before, I felt that we could go even further. It wasn't just about the most efficient fight in the world, but a very powerful tool for transforming lives.

Western society, while living at the height of comfort and practicality, carries the weight of moving away from values and virtues.

We see a youth accustomed to the law of least effort and addicted to dopamine, a group that doesn't value things and has the false idea that achievements won't be lost.

But the world tells us a different story and that's why we always need to be focused on the next move. After all, the fight is only won when the judge raises his arm.

Solving one problem alerts us to the next, and we must prepare ourselves. The desire to avoid setbacks often causes people to hide and not take risks in the hope that their comfort zone will last a little longer. This idea makes us leave our fate in the hands of others, using excuses – excuses, the denial of guilt – and not taking responsibility for what happens to us.

Jiu-Jitsu doesn't allow us to shirk responsibility for our actions – your mistakes are yours. Analyzing them, training and practicing constantly are the only way to correct them. Complaining doesn't help; justifying yourself doesn't generate any empathy in an environment where people generally pay the price of defeat and deal with failure in a positive way – by reflecting, improving, working.

CHAPTER 33

Obstacles

I was already training without any limitations when I started to feel a twinge in my right hip. Dr. Dantas had warned me about wear and tear on both sides, but at the time only the left side was bothering me. Maybe I'd never have to do anything with my right side and I thought that, as it was more flexible, I wouldn't really have any problems.

Once again, the solution would be surgery – total hip arthroplasty. With a new prosthesis, would I be able to train jiu-jitsu again?

I didn't wait another second. Once diagnosed, I booked the procedure with complete confidence that it would work. The doctor did another impeccable job and, just over 24 hours later, I was home.

So I programmed myself for an even better recovery: I already knew the protocol, the points where I would need to limit myself and wait for the healing to take place. I knew that the first week would be difficult, but then it would get better quickly.

Discipline and dedication paid off and, within a month, I was discharged and back on the mats to begin my full recovery.

We all wish we didn't have problems and, when we get out of one, we believe we deserve a rest before facing the next one. However, this is a romantic view that is detached from reality. We face many difficulties that are beyond our will or control, and mishaps can happen completely at random. We have to be ready. To do this, we put ourselves in a place of constant development – regardless of the moment, my day must be geared towards self-evolution, towards my best version. This is what prepares me for the imponderable, the unknown, the random.

The concept of antifragility needs to be put into our lives, and there's only one way to do that: by practicing the things that are right.

We have to stop being slaves to our addictions and desires, which are always related to pleasure and comfort, and start seeing the importance of sacrifice. It imposes on us long-term rewards rather than immediate pleasure, and that's what we need to get used to.

The beauty of planting lies in the reward of harvesting.

In the struggle, we see a fortress being built up over the years by the right attitudes, by the search for knowledge and health care. We can't win by luck or random movements, even if that doesn't seem to be true if we look at it in a short time frame.

The value of sacrifice is brilliantly translated in a beautiful speech by the then president of the United States, Theodore Roosevelt, at the Sorbonne University in Paris on April 23, 1910. The text became known as *Man in the Arena* and I transcribe it below:

It's not the critic who matters; not the man who points out how the strong man falters, or where those who have achieved something could have done it better. The credit belongs to the man who finds himself in the arena, whose face is stained with dust, sweat and blood; the one who strives bravely; who makes mistakes, who encounters one setback after another, for there is no effort without mistakes and failures; the one who strives to achieve his deeds, who knows great enthusiasm, great devotion, who gives himself to a noble cause; who, in the best of cases, knows the triumph of great achievement in the end, and who, in the worst of cases, if he fails, at least fails by daring greatly, so that his place will never be with those cold and timid souls who know neither victory nor failure.

CHAPTER 34

Jiu-Jitsu in the *hype*

Jiu-Jitsu is currently experiencing perhaps its most influential moment. The IBJJF's work to promote the sport around the world has led countless teachers to set up their academies and bring the art to millions of people. Some have become great ambassadors, reinforcing exactly what I have been defending throughout this book and the forty years I have dedicated to the art.

To bring Jiu-Jitsu to as many people as possible, to make it understood not just as an efficient fight, but as a tool to help solve problems and help us all evolve as a society, to promote it as a vehicle to help develop virtues, capable of taking the practitioner out of their comfort zone and awakening their courage, their ethics and their awareness of long-term construction.

Today, the martial art is reaching people through admirable personalities, *e.g.* the American communicator and black belt Joe Rogan, who leads the world's largest podcast with an average audience of eleven million viewers; Jocko Willink, best-selling author and lecturer; the Brazilian model Gisele Bündchen, a purple belt.

Kelly Slater, the greatest surfer of all time, publicly told all parents: "get your kids into jiu-jitsu before any sport". This list goes on and on and wherever you go these days, the martial art is becoming more and more well known.

Are all teachers prepared to meet this demand? I don't think so. We need to awaken in all practitioners, and especially in professionals, the need to take Jiu-Jitsu to their students in a broader way, to move away from the narrow vision of exclusively preparing athletes for competition, understanding that people have different goals in life and that being a competitor is something increasingly limited due to the difficulties of being a high-level athlete.

Anyone can benefit from jiu-jitsu as a development tool. Learning the philosophy that exists within the martial art is beneficial for everyone, as long as the gym knows how to separate the different groups so that everyone can enjoy the practice in the best way.

My end-of-class talks on the mat with the students, in which I always try to reinforce the concepts we've learned, began to spread on social media and with them came many invitations to give talks. One of the first came from Tallis Gomes, one of Brazil's brightest entrepreneurial minds, founder of Easy Taxi and G4 Educação. He realized that the Brazilian entrepreneur is a hero in overcoming all the country's difficulties, but that there is a window of opportunity to offer something more structured to small and medium-sized entrepreneurs. Tallis invited me to be a mentor for one of G4 Educação's programs, together with the former commander of Rio de Janeiro's Special Operations Battalion, Colonel Maurílio Nunes. The idea was to address leadership under extreme pressure.

We ran several very successful classes, and this opened other doors for me to continue as a speaker and take jiu-jitsu even further. Above all, it gave me another important insight, through a sensational *network* promoted with care by the G4 team.

The conversations during breaks are always very rich and, in one of them, a student who was curious about the Alliance's business model made the following suggestion: let's buy a percentage of all the affiliates, so that we can better control the delivery of the service and protect the brand.

Scott Galloway had already introduced me to the term "*freezing point*", which refers to the extent to which we accept the differences between our schools. The higher, the better for the brand.

This was on my mind for a while and I finally decided that we should move into a new business vertical. The aim was to raise the bar in delivering jiu-jitsu in very nice and pleasant "stores", as well as creating a source of income for the company. The *flagships,* the model gyms of this new vision, help us along this path.

I then thought back to a conversation I had a few years ago with a student who had moved to London, when we envisioned the possibility of setting up an Alliance there. I thought it would be the best opportunity to start the plan – having a model gym in the center of the world would be sensational. The negotiations progressed and he decided to do the deal with me. I explained that it wouldn't be exactly with me, but with Alliance as a company, and that the partners were very excited.

Within a few months, we had a property that perfectly met all our aspirations. Situated in the Chelsea neighborhood 30 meters from the River Thames, it was beautiful, and we handed over the architectural mission to my wife, Carolina, who understands all the needs of a jiu-jitsu academy and like me wanted to raise the level of delivery in our schools.

The installation wasn't easy, the permissions and negotiations with the landlord took a long time, but we kept going because we knew that one day everything would work out.

In the meantime, an 820-square-meter property came up in the Jardins district of São Paulo, the perfect place for another Alliance *flagship*. But I couldn't, for ethical reasons, sell the gym to Michael and then set up another one. I needed to involve him in the process.

Although he was a little suspicious and not so sure, he trusted us and took over the management of Alliance Jardins, which became the first model gym to open in February 2023. Within two months, we reached *breakeven* and, within a year and a half, the 460-student mark.

In July of the same year, we finally opened the Alliance London jewel, with two of our best teachers: Henrique Rezende, or "Piuhim", and Renata Marinho.

We ended up realizing the big problem in our growth: the difficulty in getting qualified teachers.

A few years earlier, Gigi created the Alliance Institute with the idea of giving boys and girls from Rio de Janeiro's communities opportunities to train and compete. With supporters, the project worked for a while. However, with his move to the USA, we saw the need to reorganize the institute to meet the necessary demands of the competition team and, above all, to build what we felt was fundamental to our growth, the training of jiu-jitsu professionals.

The athletes would be provided with excellent technical development and financial support so that they could reach their maximum. At the same time, they would understand jiu-jitsu to the full, learn to teach using our methodology, study gym management and dedicate themselves to understanding "people". This was totally in line with what I believe to be the best formula – doing something for others and benefiting ourselves as well.

Thus, the Alliance Institute no longer aims just to help disadvantaged young people, but to pave the way for them to make a real living out of jiu-jitsu and to help us continue on our mission to expand around the world. It's a long and difficult process, like anything worthwhile.

I turned to ISG, a company that specializes in projects funded by the Sports Incentive Law, and they explained how the fundraising process works, as well as the responsibilities behind what we were idealizing. We structured the Alliance

Brazilian Jiu-Jitsu Institute to comply with the law and created the "*Fly high*" program, which has benefited 24 athletes.

We split into two groups led by teachers Mário Reis in Porto Alegre and Michael Langhi in São Paulo, and entered one of the most complicated phases: the search for sponsorship. It was time to do what I like least, ask. For a good cause, I went ahead.

The law requires the company to be under the real profit regime, which already excludes most small and medium-sized companies. In addition, they can only invest up to 1% – in the second year the law was in force, it was changed to 2% – of the amount they would pay in tax to the government in the form of a tax waiver, in other words, they need to have profits in the millions to be able to make any difference.

In the specific case of our project, to finance 24 athletes traveling to compete in the *Grand Slam*, as well as housing and training, the cost would be more than R$1,500,000.00. Another difficult battle.

With this mission ahead of me, the importance of relationships and the value of an almost magical word – credibility – has once again become clear. I try to teach my students, and especially the young people at the institute, the lesson I learned from my father at an early age: be trustworthy, don't negotiate your word and your honor, build a solid image over the years.

In a lifetime, many people are co-opted by the convenient. Opportunities that seem like a shortcut give immediate rewards, which can bring good money or even a more prestigious position. Often, you know it's not the right thing to do, because you often bypass concepts that shouldn't be flexible, or you step on someone on the way up – even the one you helped, the famous ingratitude.

All the temptations we are subjected to throughout our lives force us to make sometimes difficult decisions, but they also shape our character and build credibility, one of the most admirable values we can find in people.

I started talking to people who I thought might be able to help. Normally these sponsorships happen in the last quarter of the year, because of the companies' fiscal closures.

We got three major backers for our first year of the project: BTG, Fundo Gávea and PetroRio. The total amount raised was almost half of the initial project, and we needed to adjust the costs – which is quite common in this type of incentivized action. At the beginning of the year, we realized that we would only have enough money for the World Championships and we wouldn't even be able to finance the other tournaments – the European, Pan-American and Brazilian.

We didn't control the deadlines or the time of all the people involved, a very bureaucratic process. We ran as fast as we could, but we were very inexperienced and came up against several obstacles we hadn't counted on.

We had a good chunk of money, the project had been approved in Brasilia and we believed that everything would work out. However, time was tight and we still had to go through the Sports Secretary's committee to release the funds. Without that, nothing would happen.

The meeting was scheduled for the last possible date, a few weeks before the World Championhsips, but our project wasn't put on the table. We had run out of money.

Our athletes were training with a dedication that filled us with pride, and this news was a cold shower. Half the team probably wouldn't have made it without the sponsorship.

We decided to bear the costs for the Association and, if possible, we would then pay it back when the funding was released – and we didn't even know that would never happen. The most important thing was to take our full team and win back the title we had lost in 2021.

The World Championships were back at the Long Beach University Pyramid in California, a traditional venue since the championships left Brazil and moved to the USA. Our team had been competing at the pyramid since 2007 and we had won no less than ten editions there, after the two championships in Brazil in 1998 and 1999.

We competed with the full team. We were champions for the 13th time.

CHAPTER 35

Jiu-Jitsu off the mats

Ever since I chose to make jiu-jitsu my life, I understood that I would always need to be ready for the inevitable transitions in order to remain relevant in an embryonic market for which I saw enormous growth potential. Dedication, study and quality, and knowing that spaces would be limited due to the size of the niche, are other points that I always took into consideration. As I explained earlier, any failure in the process would cost a lot.

If I had made a mistake in the first transition – from competitive athlete to teacher – my life in jiu-jitsu would have been much shorter. Likewise, being successful in this movement was a guarantee of just a little more time, a few years perhaps. Without the knowledge of management, and consequently leadership and team building, you can't build a successful academy.

Change is always difficult, because it carries the weight of becoming the last in line for that new role. We've already talked about this in this book. I was an athlete, four times world champion, and I became a weak teacher. Then I learned and evolved, delivering better quality lessons to my students. Later, I became a gym manager, a job in which I was a joke.

Once again, I had to study. At that time, as well as being a teacher, I was the leader of the competition team – a role in which I had to deal with different egos and desires.

Doing several things at once has taught me to live the stages more smoothly. I managed to become the executive of a company, Alliance, where I have the duty to walk a successful path in the mission of impacting people's lives through the art I have chosen.

Over the course of more than forty years of jiu-jitsu, I've experienced a series of situations that have shaped the person I am and reinforced the upbringing I've had. However, my way of communicating the motivations behind my attitudes and feelings wasn't very clear. Reading and studying gradually changed that.

The more I understood how important it is to pursue a life of virtue, the more I related it to the concepts of jiu-jitsu. The code of honor adopted by the world's great leaders is directly related to what I live on the mat every day, even today.

The stoic virtues – courage, wisdom, temperance and justice – and the cardinal virtues – prudence, justice, fortitude and temperance – fit exactly with the way I try to live.

△

CHAPTER 36

The virtues

COURAGE

Fight with honor and hard work.

(Alliance Culture)

This is perhaps my favorite virtue, because I understand that all the others derive from it. Without it, nothing is possible.

Normally, the first thing that comes to mind when we think of courage is fear, but it shouldn't be like that. It's just another emotion that we don't have a choice about – whether or not to feel, and when.

Things happen all around us and, more often than not, beyond our control. The central question is how to react to it.

As I see it, it's as if we were at a fork in the road and needed to decide which path to take. The first is to confront the causes of fear, the second is cowardice, running away and trying to hide from what causes us discomfort.

We could draw a parallel here with the hero's journey, a symbolic structure that traces the cycle of a sequence of events, often used for works of literature and cinema. Described in Joseph Campbell's book, *The Hero with a Thousand Faces*, it represents a call to adventure in an ordinary life. Heading into the unknown and the uncertain, escaping the limits of what is safe, requires a considerable amount of courage.

And only after that does a virtuous journey begin, in which mentors are found, challenges are overcome, defeats are felt and transformations are necessary for real learning, in order to see the purpose of life.

On the road to cowardice, people are often tempted with the excuse of not facing up, in the hope that they can hide from the problem that is bothering them. I don't think this is a good choice for a number of reasons.

Initially, it doesn't solve the problem, which can – and invariably will – cause another encounter with the same situation. It's like postponing the resolution by allowing the issue to grow and strengthen.

Next, we won't be dealing with virtuous people who are willing to take a risk in the name of something they believe in, who understand the difficulty of coping and are willing to extend a helping hand. They are usually empathetic and sensitive to difficulties.

On the road to cowardice, we find envy, laziness and cheating. Those who travel this road shirk responsibility and have self-protection as their main value. They don't give of themselves for anything or anyone, so they are the exact opposite of the virtues I described about the road of courage.

There's a well-known saying in fighting circles: "A day red with blood is better than a life yellow with fear". It refers to those who run away from the fight rather than face possible defeat.

Facing problems with courage doesn't mean being inconsequential and irrational, but believing that it's possible to live without controlling our emotions is a dangerous utopia, as you run the risk of becoming a coward – the worst characteristic a human being can have.

Courage can be trained quite often. Once, I was walking with my dog, an English mastiff called Milka, and was on my way home when I noticed a pit bull running towards us, unleashed and clearly coming to attack us. I lived with many animals of this breed during my youth in Rio de Janeiro, some trained to fight and others extremely docile. In general, they are friendly with humans, but not so much with other dogs.

I jerked Milka's collar to make her aware of the threat, but the other animal was quicker and lunged at her, biting her. Milka had the reflex to turn her body away from her attacker, who bit her on the upper side of the hip. I heard the mastiff's cry of pain and the pit bull's growl.

Once the bite was firm, the animal would start pulling and tearing at Milka. I had no doubts: I grabbed the pit bull's cheeks and pushed them against the mastiff's body so that it couldn't tear or move its mouth to a vital place. While he tried to pull back, I pushed forward and Milka screamed in pain.

Long seconds passed before the owner, my neighbor, arrived at the scene completely lost and not knowing what to do. I told him to hold on to his dog's hind legs, as it would lose traction and perhaps come loose. He did as I said, but it was no use. The pit bull didn't let go of the bite, but he was forced to stretch out his previously shrunken body. As it did so, I realized that its neck was stretched out right in front of me. I wrapped my arms as tightly as I could, released my left hand and landed the tightest, strongest rear naked choke of my life. I felt the pit bull go limp in my arms until it released my dog.

In a split second, I assessed the situation. With its life in my hands, I could squeeze it or simply let it go. Killing an animal that was obviously acting out of its nature is unreasonable and goes against all my principles. I shouted for the owner to give me the collar and released the stranglehold, quickly putting it on the still limp animal.

It's not hard to see that it was jiu-jitsu that gave me the confidence and balance for yet another act of courage.

I've never come across anyone who despises this virtue. So why is it so hard to find? Why have some begun to believe that it is no longer necessary?

Perhaps the answer lies once again in the many facilities that the modern world provides, with which individuals have come to understand that human beings will have everything they need, at any time, at their disposal. For this to happen, however, a series of certain and predictable events are required.

I don't like thinking about this perfect world, and I don't think it's possible either. If we don't even have the ability to control what's around us, what makes us think we can control everything else?

I prefer to rely on my ability to react to unpredictable things, which will always and invariably happen. Becoming adaptable is undoubtedly a condition for survival and, much more than that, a rule for a good life.

Being adaptable means not being so vulnerable, being adaptable means security. To do this, we need to practice, to get used to mistakes and failures, to correct our course without regret, to learn from each defeat. Losing is part of the process, but for those who practice, it is never the destination. Over time, we'll start to win. Difficulties will always exist, but we'll get to know them well and won't be bothered by them anymore.

Victories happen, and we learn from them. If we take it for granted, we'll be disappointed. Only practice corrects and teaches.

I hear people wishing they had started something a long time ago, or simply that they hadn't stopped doing something they liked. How many meet me and say: "Gee, if I hadn't stopped, I'd be a black belt by now".

"If" is a conditional conjunction often used by those who give up on things, and this kind of thinking doesn't help much.

There is an Arab story about a pilgrim who was walking through the scorching desert and wanted some shade. Exhausted, he came across an old man planting a seed, and asked why he was doing this, since the tree should have been planted twenty years ago. The elder agreed and said: "Yes, twenty years ago would have been the best time, because we would have had shade and could have rested a bit and protected ourselves from the heat. But the second best time is now. From now on, other people, and maybe even you who are still young, will be able to enjoy it."

We mustn't boycott ourselves. Doing is the best remedy for all situations. Not doing means being at the mercy of the actions of others, being a mere spectator of life.

We must practice, be active and be in constant movement, only then will we find our own path and purpose.

***

TEMPERANCE

Always use kindness as the main tool in resolving conflicts.
(Alliance Culture)

Reflection ahead of reaction.

There are many difficult situations in jiu-jitsu. Let's imagine a scenario where the opponent is on my back – the most dominant position in jiu-jitsu – with an arm around my neck, ready to strangle me. Calmness under pressure is essential for a successful defense. However, I can't want to escape and balance the fight with just one technique. To get to that point, a series of mistakes and wrong decisions were made. To undo this whole process with just one move is an almost childish desire and quite out of touch with reality.

In every moment of difficulty, however hard it may seem, there is at least one action in the right direction. Sometimes it's small, just enough to keep us from being strangled.

A technique in the right direction forces my opponent to try and recover lost ground, and gives me another chance to use another move to get further away from the danger, as well as forcing the opponent to open up even more in an attempt to regain control. Eventually, it creates enough space to get out of that situation and rebalance the fight.

The main point is to keep your emotions under control and focus only on what is possible, not what is desirable. Fighting to win that battle needs to be your only goal. If you can focus on that, you'll receive the consequence of a job well done and you'll be motivated for the next step, and so on.

This whole process is an ally in the fight against a disease that is so prevalent in our society today: anxiety, which is nothing more than the projection of events into an uncertain future. Having the power to focus on what is possible and necessary at a given moment forces us to work in the present. I have no doubt that temperance is the greatest ally in becoming a calmer and less anxious person.

***

WISDOM

Studying, qualifying and sharing.

(Alliance Culture)

Being in constant search of evolution is a basic condition for a purposeful life. Having the humility to recognize that we know little in the face of the world's knowledge brings the awareness that we must travel the road of study, certain that we will never reach its end, armed with the curiosity to see how far we can go.

Humanity is full of great thinkers, great leaders, writers, intellectuals, etc. There are countless sources of study, but the big question is: where to start? Is it too late?

It's never too late to try to improve or to change in search of a life of virtues.

In his book *From strength to strength,* author Arthur Brooks emphasizes that life follows its course of transitions and we must constantly rediscover new challenges, learning new things, feeling the rewards of our efforts, and this has absolutely nothing to do with age or even what we do for a living.

Your career doesn't have to be a straight line, and you should just challenge yourself to be productive, preferably by doing something that makes a difference to the lives of others.

There probably isn't just one starting point, although there are good references and not so good ones. One thing seems obvious: we can't escape the study of philosophy – the "love of wisdom".

In a way, all of today's authors have been nourished by the ideas of the great thinkers and philosophers of the past. Therefore, if you investigate the sources of what you read – and I hope you do – you will be drawn to the original thinker, which may allow you to have a slightly different interpretation of what you were reading before.

I don't believe that wisdom lies more in books than in practice. In fact, I think this understanding is quite dangerous, as it could lead us down a common path these days, that of the intellectual bureaucrats, those who have read everything and never done anything, never taken any risks, and never paid the price for any mistakes. Our society is infested with them.

Thomas Sowell, in his classic and wonderful book *Intellectuals and Society*, puts it this way: "The confidence generated by superior academic knowledge can conceal from the members of the elite themselves the extent of their ignorance and misconceptions." Beware of knowledge without practice.

So I ask you in the world,
Is the book or wisdom more intelligent?

To respond to these verses sung by Marisa Monte ("Gentileza"), I'm going to bring up a reflection by Plato. In *The Republic*, he explains to his interlocutor Adiamanthus the difficulty of seeking wisdom:

We know that ease of learning, good memory, liveliness of mind, perspicacity, youthful passion and magnificence, and all the qualities that go with them, rarely lend themselves to developing in combination in an intellect that is ready for an orderly, tranquil and entirely stable life, because individuals who possess the first of these attributes are driven by their liveliness of mind wherever chance leads them, and are totally devoid of stability. On the other hand, those who are stable, not fickle, who are not easily frightened in battle, and who are more useful because they are more reliable, display an identical conduct when it comes to learning. It is difficult to rouse them to study, they learn with difficulty, as if numb, and they are markedly sleepy and yawn every time they have to make an effort to learn. And yet, we say that an individual needs to have a good and generous portion of both temperaments combined, otherwise they won't be fit for the most rigorous education, honors or governing.

With this understanding, it seems clear to me that we should try to complete ourselves in the search for wisdom, mixing both practice and theoretical studies. We will realize that, at certain stages, our temperament will lead us in a certain direction. If we wish to become more capable people, we will need to strive to achieve this combination. The upside is that we have our whole lives to do it.

I hear many people say that they're old and can't do this or that anymore, or that they don't have the motivation to learn anything because "there won't be time". If you are one of these people, or know someone who fits this profile, allow me to give you some examples from my own life.

Since I was fifteen, jiu-jitsu was the only activity to which I dedicated myself 100%. Everything that could, in one way or another, hinder my performance, I didn't do. Everything that took up my training time, I didn't do.

I've spent a lot of years dedicated to the path I've chosen, and I don't regret it for a second. However, as I grew out of my peak performance, I made room for other activities. I wasn't competing anymore, so if I got injured doing another sport, it wouldn't cost me so much.

I started *snowboarding* when I was forty-eight. Then I had to have two hip surgeries. I took it up again at the age of fifty-three, and even started surfing, which has been extremely fun.

A more disciplined reading routine has brought quality into my life. Doing new things keeps me hungry to learn, and moves the development of my virtues forward. This is how I see a life of wisdom.

***

JUSTICE

Always do the right thing and never the convenient thing.
(Alliance Culture)

This is probably the phrase I most identify with in Alliance culture, as it represents what is right and seeks to keep us away from the temptations that invariably appear in front of us, as immediate advantages that jeopardize our future.

A study carried out at Stanford by psychologist Walter Mischel consisted of placing pre-school children on one side of a table and a *marshmallow* on the other. He offered them the candy and told them they could eat it, but that there was a catch. Then he would leave the room for fifteen minutes. When he returned, if they hadn't eaten, he would give them another *marshmallow* as a reward.

Most couldn't wait and ate the candy. He followed the children in the study for many years, and realized that those who were able to resist grew up healthier and happier, earned more and had better grades in the school aptitude tests carried out by American universities. He also looked at issues such as family security, socio-economic situation, etc., but the main conclusion is simple: good things come to those who know how to wait, to those who work, sacrifice and even suffer.

This leads us to reflect on how much we are willing to fight against our addictions, which can also be understood as the comfort and ease with which we are accustomed.

Forcing ourselves into some amount of restriction seems to me to be very salutary in the development of virtues. Learning to give up the things we want in order to have access to what we really need puts us ahead of most "children" who couldn't resist a simple *marshmallow*.

Of course, each person has their own assessment of the concepts of right and wrong, often based on their culture and experience. But it's hard not to agree that right is linked to good and wrong to evil.

Therefore, a good guide to know if we are making decisions in a way that develops the virtue of justice would be to assess whether we are doing good by choosing a certain attitude, or if we are just seeking immediate pleasure in a hedonistic way.

The path is often not the easiest, as it requires courage, time and renunciation. However, truly building a legacy is only possible by following this route. And the realization of a life of virtue can be compared to absolutely no isolated pleasure, as it is man's own natural function.

CHAPTER 37

From lemon to lemonade

I believe it's easier to learn from defeats. Firstly, because the mistakes are more obvious. Then, because it becomes clear that we need to change if we want to achieve another result. After all, expecting different responses to the same attitude isn't very smart.

Many experience the need to find a culprit for failure, which is relatively easy. The world is full of excuses and, when we put this abundance together with human creativity, we really see something tempting, which feeds most people who can't deal with defeat in a positive way.

Creating opportunities out of obstacles is fundamental to constant progress. When we have a defeat, no matter how big or small, we shouldn't waste time lamenting.

There's a thought I like a lot, by an unknown author: "When you win, look in the window and share it with those you helped. When you lose, look in the mirror and find your faults".

That way, we'll always be grateful to the people who helped us achieve things. We don't do anything alone. On the other hand, we must look at our reflection to analyze our mistakes and really try to improve.

This way of thinking pushes us forward and removes the fear of challenge and uncertainty. If we believe that defeat opens the way to evolution, losing won't terrify us. On the contrary, it will free us to do the only thing that will really make us better in any area: practise.

Alliance was at a good moment. We opened our first two *flagships* – in São Paulo and London. In 2022, we won three IBJJF World Championships – the World Adult Championship, the World Masters Championship and the World No-Gi Championship – an unprecedented feat in the history of the sport. We had almost three hundred licensed schools in more than thirty countries, and our business continued to grow at a rate of 30% a year.

The plan to expand the *flagships* was a different challenge, because it required capital, and I had to talk to my partners. If they agreed, we would have a few options, such as doing everything with our own resources and moving slowly, or seeking external capital to work in a more structured way.

Two things pushed me towards the second alternative. The first was to think of a way out for Jacaré, who could eventually sell part of his shares to a new partner and enjoy his retirement peacefully. The other reason was to have the capital to bring in qualified people to help with this new phase of the company.

We met in Las Vegas for the traditional Masters World Championships, which these days take place as part of Jiu-Jitsu CON, a major trade fair for the sport. Like every year, we took our team and gathered our affiliates. I explained the matter to Jacaré and Gigi, who liked the idea and understood the need for structuring so that we could take the Alliance to another business level.

When I got back, I started to structure the plan, redoing the company's valuation and thinking of terms that would make the master happy, as well as being good for the company. We had an interested investor, and talks and negotiations began.

Every fight is a fight and, no matter how experienced I was in negotiations of this kind, another counterpart always teaches you something new.

The always very cordial and high-level conversations showed that we were heading in the right direction, and we agreed on the value of the company – five times higher than in 2019. I thought this was the most sensitive point, and I considered that the deal was practically closed.

The lawyers came on the scene, everything was normal and expected, and we started discussing governance and asset protection. In short, we disagreed about the management of the business. As nothing was insurmountable, we moved on.

The next step was due diligence, a real fine-tooth comb through the company to check legal and tax issues. By the time we realized it, we had been in the process for eight months, with a high level of wear and tear, and I began to wonder if it was the best course of action. In the final talks, the two parties were no longer able to compromise on anything, and we understood that it would be best not to make the move. We closed without completing the deal.

It's impossible not to feel the cold shower. We worked so hard to make it work. Looking back, I realized that our business wasn't ready, that we were coming to the end of the year and needed to turn the page urgently. So much detour of attention, among other things, distanced us from our goal.

It was very clear what we needed to do and there was no time to lose. We began the process of restructuring the business model, establishing a more modern and efficient form of management. The idea was to bring in the best practices of an *accountability model,* in which people have direct responsibility and autonomy to run their areas.

We've divided our plan into three business verticals: *flagships,* affiliates and products. In addition, we separated out the support horizontals: finance, marketing, methodology, projects, institute, etc. The need for important hires and a well-defined budget became clear.

The difference from how we operated before to our current model is striking. We are better in all aspects, we have the right people in the right places, well paid and aware of the mission.

We still have problems every day, like every company and every individual, but we are learning to look at them from a different perspective. When we don't achieve something we really want to, we have to keep going until we achieve something we never imagined we could.

CHAPTER 38

What I learned

At the age of fifty-four and with forty years of jiu-jitsu, I've learned many things, especially about the need for transitions, to reinvent ourselves and understand that each phase has its cycle, and that we need to prepare for another moment in order to remain relevant in what we decide to do.

From an early age, as I've already told you, I fell in love with jiu-jitsu; I dedicated myself as much as I could, but I always tried to look ahead. I've learned not to arouse the desire to be in the future – that takes us away from the dedication we need for the present and, consequently, for the important results we need to sow in order to reap the rewards of the future.

The maxim of Stoic philosophy is that we should focus on what is in our control, simply that. If you think about it, few things are subordinate to us. The actions we perform, our thoughts, the control of impulses and desires are the exercises to become free of our vices. If we are able to master what is subordinate to us and make choices that always look out for what is right, moral and ethical, we will be the best we can be.

On the other hand, there are things that are out of our control. With regard to these, we need to be adaptable, understand that there are unpredictable paths and deal with them at the right time.

If things go wrong, the most common reaction is to look for the culprits, but if we understand that unexpected directions are possible, we'll stop thinking about blame and continue to focus on the things that are within our reach and that can be structured.

Epithet teaches us that we improve our lives simply by not getting worse. Choices about what not to do have a huge impact on the paths we take. When we decide to get rid of something that harms us, we will no longer have to deal with the consequences of those who choose that path. It's never too late to start making wiser decisions, and past mistakes shouldn't justify resisting the search for a better path.

There is a world of temptations and things that generate immediate pleasure, but we also know that those of real value are difficult and usually take time. Work for the long term, to build your life's legacy, not for momentary and ephemeral pleasures.

What you truly become is yours and is secure; everything else is changeable and transitory. Material goods, while important achievements, are no greater than the purpose for which we do things. Never reverse the order – when the convenient appears, act for the right.

Seneca, in his masterpiece *On The Tranquility Of The Mind*, describes another fundamental and necessary point for our development: emotional control.

Fighting has put me in several situations where emotion was a scream. It's difficult to deal with some feelings, but I've learned that uncontrolled fear leads to cowardice, uncontrolled anxiety prevents concentration and the ability to evaluate the best actions to take, and uncontrolled anger leaves us completely inept, blind.

When we allow something or someone to upset us to the point of anger, we are giving them power over us. If we are unable to control our anger in order to clarify our decision-making capacity, we will invariably be in a very bad way.

If we understand that not all decisions are within our reach and we receive the negative action as just one of many possible ones, we will focus on "how to react" so that the result is better. With this exercise, we will be able to keep our anger under control, which means absolute emotional control so that no one, at any time, is able to have power over us.

Sport in general helps us to develop humility. We learn that there is always someone better than us, even though we have to be almost overbearing in our belief in our ability. In the eyes of others, we appear arrogant. At the end of the day, if we know ourselves deeply, we will know our flaws and limitations, we will be humble.

I've met athletes of all kinds, from the most snobbish, usually insecure, to the most humble, really confident. The fact is that we shouldn't be so proud of our achievements, we should keep doing them.

When we start believing what other people say, or even the character we create for the world, we start living a lie. As soon as the character no longer performs, we'll have no way of explaining that we were something else.

I like the noise of work, not self-promotion. I don't believe in the famous "pat on the shoulder". I keep working hard, and I'm never satisfied.

In this world where we're always faced with adverse situations, I've been lucky in that I've had very few injuries throughout my professional career. As I got older, my body began to show the effects of years of effort. After four surgeries, although I have recovered very well, my physical condition is not what it once was. When we have limitations in one area, we are given the opportunity to develop in another.

I understand that the world is organized independently of my will. I may not like it or simply wish it were different. And I can be grateful for the way it is, for the opportunities it gives me. That's how we see the glass as half full. Always be ready to do what needs to be done and continue on your path of evolution, whatever that may be.

Most of the time since I was nineteen, when I received my black belt, I've been the reference point for others on the mats. People came to me to ask technical questions and listen to my explanations. I've always enjoyed being a teacher, and realizing that my teachings add to the lives of others is one of the reasons I keep striving to improve.

However, we need to be wary when we are the most knowledgeable person in the room. We shouldn't rely so much on our wisdom, because it is, and always will be, insufficient. We need to surround ourselves with people who add something to us, bearing in mind that: "You're the average of the five people you hang out with the most, don't be the smartest person in the room"[40].

Exaggerate kindness. Nothing is more elegant than being kind, and nothing is more effective in resolving conflicts.

Carry with you the security and self-confidence that allow you to be the first to seek a solution to any problem. Don't raise your voice, argue calmly and technically, clarify your point of view without insisting that the other person thinks like you. Accept differences, after all, you don't have to change the world and, even if you try, you won't be able to.

Constantly seek knowledge through study and practice. It is what makes us alive and relevant, especially if it is used not only for our own benefit, but also for that of others.

My dedication to jiu-jitsu has allowed me to reach thousands of people, not to mention the many who have passed through my academy. Only 139 fighters have received a black belt from me. Many continue to train and teach the art at our school. Others have stopped training. Some remain outside the Alliance. At some point, I understood that they were ready for the mission of carrying the flag of jiu-jitsu in the best possible way. The consequence of this is an incalculable positive impact on the lives of so many other people whom I have never met in person.

---

40. Sentence of unknown authorship.

Epithet teaches us: "You are not what you have". And that goes for everything. Whether it's material goods or a black belt tied around our waist, we need to earn them every day.

I've learned that we have a finite and indefinite time on earth, which we need to make very worthwhile, no matter how long it takes. To leave our mark on this world, to inspire the people around us to do their best, to set an example of always doing the right thing, to act loyally and fairly even when no one is looking. In this way, we become the best version of ourselves.

Remember the concept of *memento mori,* reflect on death and the ephemerality of your life. When we do this, realizing that time gets shorter every day and that we may not be here tomorrow, we start to live the now in the most virtuous way we can.

I found jiu-jitsu and the study of philosophy to be a powerful combination. I practice as much as my body can handle and complete the rest by working on my intellect and studying. I follow the daily transformation of thousands of students and practitioners of this powerful martial art, but if you're reading these final lines and haven't yet practiced jiu-jitsu, you don't have to start if you don't want to. If you find another tool that helps you lead a practical and virtuous life, go for it. However, if you feel like it, look for a gym near your home and just let yourself go. You won't regret it.

Thanks

I would like to thank all the students I have worked with so far for what they have taught me in my life. Some, in particular, received their black belt from me. In them, I recognized the values that I defend and their maturity in the art.

Being a black belt means remaining open-minded about learning and, at the same time, sharing the knowledge you acquire. It means not running away from your responsibilities, facing the unknown with bravery and courage, finding a new path when the previous one is closed. It means not complaining or blaming others. It's "taking your mistakes to heart" and humbly trying again, always doing your best. It's not being content. It's being kind. It's knowing the cost of sacrifice and still doing it because you recognize its value. It's paying the price for your actions and sharing the glory with those who helped you on your journey. It's being true to your principles and values.

From the list below, those highlighted are still part of the Alliance team:

1. Ricardo "Franjinha" Miller
2. **Leandro Bordo**
3. **Pedro "Jaca" Andrade**
4. **Leo Negão**
5. Demian Maia
6. Eduardo Telles
7. **Paulo "Chimpa" Sguizzardi**
8. **Marcelo Garcia**
9. **Cassio Cardosi**
10. **Pierre Chofard**
11. **Alex Monsalve**
12. **Andre Gailey**

13. **Orlando Andrade**
14. **Rodrigo Petroni**
15. **Eduardo Miranda**
16. Cezar Takeyoshi
17. **Ricardo Delneri**
18. **Fernando "Hiccup" Di Pierro**
19. **Gustavo French**
20. **Fabbio Passos**
21. **Eduardo Bordim**
22. Fábio Romão
23. **Tarsis Humphreys**
24. **Daniel Amabile**
25. **João Manssur**
26. **Michael Langhi**
27. Beto Garcia
28. **Antônio "Batista" Peinado**
29. **Tati Tognini Garcia**
30. **Geraldo Azevedo**
31. **Felipe Pacces**
32. **Roberta Parisi**
33. **Tiago Rocha**
34. **Leo Nogueira**
35. **Sérgio Santos**
36. **Rodrigo Funaro**
37. **Henrique Resende**
38. Tommy Malmberg
39. **David Dimopoulos Said**
40. **Gabi Garcia**
41. **Henry Navorra**
42. **Eduardo Moura**
43. **Ricardo Lewandowski**
44. **Gustavo Junqueira**
45. **Gabriel Goulart**
46. **Dimitrius Souza**
47. **Helio Costa**
48. **Fabio "Bolivia" Suzuki**
49. **Daniel "Cabelinho" Nogueira**
50. Juha Järvinen
51. Terho Virrankoski
52. **Mikko Rouvali**
53. **Ricardo "Aritana Miranda"**
54. **Filipi Sagat**
55. **Ribamar Santiago**
56. **Henry Khouri**
57. **Juuso Harma**
58. **Ricardo Mesquita**
59. **Andresa Correa**
60. **Juan Kamezawa**
61. **Thomas Lisboa**
62. **José Júnior**
63. **Leo de Nigris**
64. **Kiko Alem**
65. **Jean Louis Bouquerel**
66. **Alexandre Maron**
67. **Marcelo Mora**
68. Greger Forsell
69. **Petri Kolehmainen**
70. **Fabio Caloi**
71. Carlos Santos
72. Teo Viitala
73. Ulf Ehlert
74. **Gustavo Bonelli**
75. **Luciano Tavares**
76. **Fernando Kurayama**
77. **Wolney Atalla**
78. **Olavo Torrano**

79. **Hannu Karjalainen**
80. **Matias Simonelli**
81. **Teemu Toroi**
82. **Luiz Nunes**
83. **Edson Costa**
84. **Helio Laniado**
85. **Cristian Fogaccia**
86. **Tarean Humphreys**
87. **Walter Buse**
88. **Edson Oliveira**
89. **Fernando Reis**
90. **"Spiderman**
91. **Caio Rigante**
92. **Ricardo Caloi**
93. **Felipe Nacib**
94. **Oscar Eklöf**
95. **Magda Maron**
96. **Eduard Lisboa**
97. **Marcelo Ferreira**
98. Isaque Bahiense
99. Ali Monfaradi
100. **Pablo Mesples**
101. **Flavio Junqueira**
102. **Renata Marinho**
103. **Matthew Lasco**
104. **Janne Laine**
105. **Ricardo Bezerra**
106. **Raphael Castro**
107. **Thomas Conde**
108. **Hoannes Nacib**
109. **Fernando Almeida**
110. Adam Childs
111. **Vinícius "Trator" Ferreira**
112. **Leonardo "Marcelinho" Garcia**
113. **Raimundo "Cupim" Cezar**
114. **Rafael Ramos**
115. **Maurício Cascão**
116. **Mayra Mazza**
117. **Adolpho Mello**
118. **Gabriel Bergami**
119. **Marcos "Scooby" Ribeiro**
120. Gabriel Figueiró
121. Wesley dos Santos
122. **Bruno Leite**
123. Lucas José
124. Rafael Paganini
125. Caio Paganini
126. Gustavo Maron
127. Ramon Delsin
128. **Antonio Henrique Azevedo**
129. **Gabriela Azevedo**
130. **Nataly Santos**
131. **Renato Chiusano Moran**
132. **André Schiliró**
133. **José Arnaldo Suaid**
134. **Vitor Zandona**
135. **Brenda Larissa**
136. **Stefano Virionis**
137. **Gurdip Rangi**
138. **Rodrigo Kurayama**
139. **David Bernacca**

Many other names have influenced my career in some way. Throughout this book, I mention just a few of the many fighters who have taught me something. My special thanks go to the following colleagues:

1. Adilson Lima
2. Alexandre Gigi Paiva
3. Alípio Amaral
4. Amaury Bitetti
5. André Galvão
6. Andrezinho
7. Antonio Peinado
8. Bernardo Faria
9. Roberto Motta
10. Bobby Armijo
11. Bráulio Carsalade
12. Bruno Malfacine
13. Caio Rigante
14. Carlos de Tarso
15. Carlos Gracie *(in memoriam)*
16. Carlos Soneca Machado
17. Carlson Gracie *(in memoriam)*
18. Cassio Cardoso
19. Crolin Gracie
20. Daniel Gracie
21. Dedé Pederneiras
22. Demian Maia
23. Denilson Maia LL
24. Eduardo Telles
25. Eugênio Tadeu LL
26. Fernando Tererê
27. Gabriel Goulart
28. Gastão Gracie *(in memoriam)*
29. Gastão Gracie Jr.
30. George Gracie, the Ginger Cat *(in memoriam)*
31. Heleno de Freitas
32. Hélio Gracie *(in memoriam)*
33. Hélio Santana
34. Hélio Vígio *(in memoriam)*
35. Henrique Rezende
36. Hugo Duarte LL
37. Jean Jacques Machado
38. Jerry Bohlander
39. Jessé Rodrigues
40. João Alberto Barreto
41. Leo Negão
42. Leo Vieira
43. Leonardo Nogueira
44. Lucas Lepri
45. Ricardo Libório
46. Sérgio Malibu
47. Manimal
48. Marcelo Behring *(in memoriam)*
49. Marcelo Gurgel
50. Marcelo Mendes LL
51. Marcelo Ribeiro

52. Marcio Feitosa
53. Marco Ruas LL
54. Mário Reis
55. Mark Coleman
56. Mark Kerr
57. Masahiko Kimura *(in memoriam)*
58. Mauricio
59. Michael Langhi
60. Michael Maia
61. Michael Patchouli
62. Mitsuyo Maeda *(in memoriam)*
63. Murilo Bustamante
64. Oswaldo Gracie *(in memoriam)*
65. Pat Smith
66. Paul Varelans
67. Cloth feet
68. Peck
69. Pedro Carvalho
70. Pedro Hemetério *(in memoriam)*
71. Fernando Pinduka
72. Ralph Gracie
73. King Zulu
74. Reila Gracie
75. Renata Marinho
76. Renzo Gracie
77. Reyson Gracie
78. Ricardo Arona
79. Ricardo Caloi
80. Ricardo De La Riva
81. Ricardo Franjinha Miller
82. Rickson Gracie
83. Ricco Rodriguez
84. Rillion Gracie
85. Roberto Godoi
86. Roger Gracie
87. Rolls Gracie *(in memoriam)*
88. Rolls Gracie Jr.
89. Romero Jacaré
90. Royler Gracie
91. Rubens Cobrinha Charles
92. Ryan Gracie
93. Saulo Ribeiro
94. Sérgio Bolão Souza
95. Sérgio Moraes
96. Ken Shamrock
97. Vitor Shaolin
98. Sylvio Behring
99. Tank Abbott
100. Tarsis Humphreys
101. Marcelo Mendes "Telo"
102. Toninho
103. Roberto Traven
104. Waldemar Santana
105. Wallid Ismail
106. Wendell Alexandre
107. Yukio Kato
108. Zé Mário Sperry

The stories go that about a century ago, Mitsuyo Maeda, Count Koma, arrived in Belém do Pará and was welcomed by Gastão Gracie. As a way of showing his gratitude, he offered to teach jiu-jitsu to Gastão's eldest son, Carlos. This is how jiu-jitsu was born in Brazil.

Today, I feel fulfilled for being part of the great Alliance family, for having helped so many people find the path of human virtue, and for having worked to make jiu-jitsu seen as what it really is.

For me, jiu-jitsu is much more than a fight. It's an art, a passion and a philosophy of life.

Follow LVM Editora

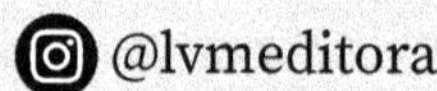

Visit: www.clubeludovico.com.br

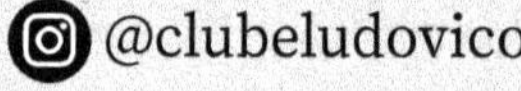

This edition was prepared by LVM Editora with typography Source Serif Pro and Acumin Pro ExtraCondensed, in March 2025.

www.ingramcontent.com/pod-product-compliance
Lightning Source LLC
LaVergne TN
LVHW040408280525
812275LV00010B/606

* 9 7 8 6 5 5 0 5 2 2 7 2 8 *